Purpose, Passion, and God

Awakening to the Deepest Meaning of Life

JANICE R. DUNLAP
PURPOSE, PASSION, & *God*
Awakening to the deepest meaning of life

Logos Publications, Inc.
Manila
2007

The Society of the Divine Word (SVD) is an international missionary congregation of priests and brothers serving in more than fifty countries all over the world. Through the Logos Publications, the SVD in the Philippines aims to foster the apostolate of the printed word in the biblical, theological, catechetical and pastoral fields in order to promote justice, peace and human development. The opinions expressed by the authors do not necessarily reflect those of the SVD community.

Published by   Logos Publications, Inc.
                 1916 Oroquieta St., Sta. Cruz, Manila
All Rights Reserved
Printed in the Republic of the Philippines

ISBN-10: 1-58595-547-7
ISBN 978-1-58595-547-3
Library of Congress Catalog Card Number: 2005934287

Contents

Introduction

"Vocation" is a popular word these days. You find it in titles of books, in descriptions of personal enrichment workshops, in career development materials, and entire seminars are based on it. According to many guidance professionals, finding your vocation is the key to happiness and fulfillment, personal satisfaction and growth. It's about your place in the world, your unique niche. It's about your job, your career, your lifework. In short, it's all about you.

In reality, it's not.

Vocation—the original, authentic Christian type—is not about your needs, your wants, your wishes. It is not about finding career fulfillment (although it can certainly include that), nor is it about self-fulfillment (although that too may happen in the course of living one's vocation). It's not about finding happiness or making money. On the contrary, it may include poverty and suffering, sacrifice and self-abandonment. It is definitely a process, and it's certainly time-consuming, but it's not something you go looking for, or something you find, because you've already got it.

You just have to know what you're looking at.

Vocation is a theological concept and truth that is deeply rooted in the example of Jesus himself and foundational to the Christian faith. It is about the relationship between God and the individual, about God calling the person to participate in the divine plan of God. For each of us, vocation is the expression of this relationship and participation, grounded in and conditioned by the concrete circumstances of our lives. Understood in all its rich theological implications, vocation is a passionate and powerful awakening to the deepest meaning of life. As the earliest Christians experienced it, it is the Way, the Truth, and the Life. Today, for those who know what they are seeing, vocation is the way each of us embodies Jesus Christ in our world.

In recent years there has been a surging interest in the spirituality of work. Fueled by the human need to find meaning in life, many people have focused on their jobs and their careers as potent sources of self-fulfillment and spiritual definition. In response to this interest, a veritable industry has emerged, one that offers a range of assistance to individuals seeking to enhance their experience of the spiritual dimension of employment. Opportunities abound: self-help books, seminars, and conferences regularly attract large crowds. In some of the best programs, personality assessments and career counseling have joined forces with spiritual directors and faith-based vocational planning to help individuals sort out personal priorities and goals.

Drawing on the resources of varied religious traditions, both new and ancient tools for self-knowledge, such as the Enneagram, have become popular means of reflecting on the ways individuals experience spirituality in the workplace. Many churches sponsor support groups for people interested in exploring their spiritual connections to the work they do. The result of all these efforts has been an increased awareness of the relationship between work, spirituality, and personal identity. To arrive at a theological understanding of Christian vocation, however, additional elements need to be considered: the example of Jesus, the record of the New Testament, the development of theological thought, and the lived experience of faith-filled people.

As a Christian, your vocation is encoded in your life from the moment of your baptism. Even a superficial reading of the Acts of the Apostles testifies to this. Baptized in the Holy Spirit, the early Christians possessed an enormous energy and confidence in what they were doing. Separated from the earthly Jesus by only a matter of years, these first Christians were able to keep alive a clear vision of his model of living. As centuries passed, however, the simple example and directives of Jesus became heavily weighted down with increasing layers of theological interpretation and cultural assimilation. As a result, we find ourselves today with an accumulation of conceptions and corruptions of what vocation really means. From the once clear stream of Jesus' example, we have arrived at a muddy pool of confused expectations that obscures not only the meaning of vocation, but the meaning of our lives as well.

So how do we filter out the unnecessary, the incorrect, and the useless accretions that have attached themselves to vocation? How do we find again the fresh, living water that Jesus promised us, and how do we use that water to uncover the vocation already embedded in our lives?

I propose we develop a theologically correct anatomy of vocation—a model that will help us identify and understand the parts of vocation and how they interact to produce our personal experience of vocation. To accomplish this, we will do four things:

1. examine how our popular understandings of vocation are incomplete by reviewing the historical development of the theological concept;

2. construct a model of vocational development based on the record of Jesus' experience as witnessed in the New Testament;

3. investigate the individual components of the model and their operational dynamics through selected case studies; and

4. explore ways that we, as contemporary Christians, can use that model to recover not only our Christian vocations, but find new direction and meaning in our lives.

In the course of our project, I hope you also discover what I have experienced as a result of reflection on the material in this book: a soul-deep appreciation for your place in the world and the people who share it with you, a fresh (and refreshing) perspective on your daily tasks, and a new desire to unearth the passion and purpose of God already living in you.

CHAPTER 1

History

When people speak of vocation today, they often use the word interchangeably with job, career, lifework, occupation, or profession. Originally springing from the same Latin root as "voice," vocation implies a calling or summons from either an internal or external source. In addition, vocation—especially in the Christian tradition—connotes the choice of a religious lifestyle as a response to God's unique invitation to each individual. Faced with these multiple variations on a theme, it is no wonder most of us are hard-pressed to clearly articulate what vocation is. In order to clarify our understanding, we need to examine the theological meaning and usage of the word, beginning with its appearance in St. Paul's letters in the New Testament. Then we will briefly trace the development of the concept of vocation from the time of the early Christian community to our current day. We will also note some important understandings of the concept that have emerged (and later disappeared) along the way.

The Call to Christ
To be completely accurate, the word "vocation" did not appear in

Paul's original missives—it was the Latin translator of his texts who used the word *vocatio* in the place of Paul's Greek word *klesis*, or call (*God and the Common Life*, p. 17). Keeping that in mind, we will save the use of the word "vocation" for later and remain focused on Paul's word for "call," hoping thereby to more closely observe his meaning. By pointing out this distinction, we can also more carefully delineate the development of the concept of vocation, which begins with Paul's *klesis* but grows over time to include additional theological meanings.

Klesis, or call, was Paul's word of choice when he referred to God's singling out the individual to come to faith in Christ. He "saved us and called us," he instructs his readers in his second letter to Timothy, "with a holy calling, not according to our works but according to his own purpose and grace. This grace was given to us in Christ Jesus" (2 Tim 1:9). It is this meaning of call that is foundational not only to a theology of Christian vocation, but to a comprehensive understanding of Christian identity itself.

God calls the individual to a personal relationship in Jesus Christ. Paul testifies to this truth every time he begins a letter, identifying himself as "called to be an apostle" or "a slave of Christ Jesus." In so doing, he follows the traditional form of identification for a first-century Jew by naming the most important patriarchal relationship in his life, but with a twist: instead of naming his male relatives, he identifies himself with Christ. Clearly, Paul's identity has been recast in his relationship with Christ by virtue of his call from God.

In a similar fashion, the early Christians experienced their new identities as a call that required them to leave behind their previous lives. Forsaking the religious traditions in which they had been raised, converts were dependent on the Christian communities they joined, not only for their moral formation, but also for their personal sense of identification. This need to create supportive communities for the converts was so imperative for the first two centuries of Christianity that community formation was the primary task of the infant Church (*The Origins of Christian Morality*, p. 150). During this time, the Greek word *ekklesia*, meaning "those who are called," came to mean the Christian assemblies that held themselves apart from the surrounding cultures. In this context, we find another key to a theology of Christian vocation: call has a communal dimension. Just as the early Christians found themselves to be joined in relationship with one another as a basic component of their identity, so too each person's individual call affected the community as a whole. To illustrate this organic unity of the community of believers Paul relied on the metaphor of the body: "For as in one body we have many members, and not all the members have the same function, so we, who are many, are one body in Christ, and individually we are members one of another" (Rom 12:4–5).

Looking again at Scripture, it also becomes evident that Paul's *klesis* was typically coupled with purpose. In his letter to the Romans, he says he is "called to be an apostle, set apart for the gospel of God" (Rom 1:1). Later, in the same letter, he remarks that "all things work together for good for those who love God, who are called according to his purpose" (Rom 8:28). Repeatedly in his correspondence, Paul exhorts his readers to focus on their holy calling. What that particular call required, however, depended on the interpretation of the community to which the individual belonged.

Scholarly research in the last few decades has shed much light on the historical circumstances and attitudes of the various assemblies who were the original hearers of the gospels. Such research enables contemporary readers to better understand the narrations and nuances that often appear vague and even meaningless to twenty-first century sensibilities. The Johannine writings of the New Testament are a good example. Produced within a community that struggled with alienation and hostility from both Jewish and non-Jewish neighbors, these texts view the world as enemy, and a holy life as one that separates the believer from the world. In 1 John 2:15, the author admonishes the community: "Do not love the world or the things in the world. The love of the Father is not in those who love the world." In the light of this instruction, it is no surprise that John's community sought refuge from the world in house churches, where they could fortify themselves with the faith they shared with other members of the sect. Their call demanded rejection of the world and an adversarial relationship with it.

Paul's audiences heard a different message. Geographically diverse, these communities had wider experiences of urban society than John's assemblies, and Paul's texts reflect that cultural diversity. Though still viewing the world in many negative ways, Paul's letters are more focused on advising the communities how to deal with concrete situations and conflicts in their distinctive social settings. His teachings address the way to live a holy life in the midst of a non-Christian culture. Whereas John's writings take a defensive position against the world, Paul's texts encourage Christians to be guided by faith in the world. The faith-filled people, in turn, were then expected to transform the world, as the "children of light" witnessing to the saving work of Christ.

The Christian call to live a holy life, then, never arrived at a consistent interpretation among the early Christians. Instead, it was an understanding that swung between differing visions, leaving the individual communities to determine if their call was to flee from the world, to do battle against it, or to participate in its transformation (*The Origins of Christian Morality*, p. 14).

The Call to the Cloister

By the time of Constantine the Christian community was in transition. No longer a persecuted collection of house churches, Christians enjoyed the prestige and privileges of status as the official religion of the Roman Empire. As a result, Christians moved into positions of responsibility and governance, including an influx of the faithful into the military.

This latter development was problematic for the community for several reasons. In keeping with the example of Jesus, the first Christians practiced an ethic of nonviolence that forbade their participation in military service. This alone, however, did not account for their exclusion from the Roman legions. Since the majority of early Christians weren't citizens of the Empire, they were ineligible to serve even had they wanted to. This fact, combined with the many moral objections of Christians to the soldierly lifestyle (i.e., lax sexual mores, emperor-worship, and other aspects of the civil religion prior to Constantine) virtually eliminated Christian participation as an option. Consequently, when Christians began to enter the military, the leaders of the Church were forced to develop new moral and theological norms that would allow its members to remain faithful to their Christian identity while accommodating a new set of societal demands.

The solution devised by the community's leaders introduced a duality. The refusal to resort to violence became the witness, and the particular *vocatio* of monks, while other members of the community were exempted from that obligation so they could exercise responsibility—including the use of arms—for the governance of secular society (*Nuclear Ethics*, p. 10).

In this way, the Christian community preserved the teaching and example of Jesus' nonviolence in a culture that accepted and practiced violence as a political and social reality. Unfortunately, it also introduced a wedge of distinction into the common witness of the members of the community. Although the Christian identity of each member remained the same, different standards applied depending on whether the individual lived inside or outside the monastery.

As time passed and Christians continued to be assimilated into the general population, this distinction became a division as monks and nuns—especially those who followed the ascetic tradition—felt themselves called to separate from the world and a

Church that had grown increasingly secular. Experienced as an inward call, this spiritual invitation led to the renunciation of all earthly ambitions and affections in the pursuit of God's friendship. By the fourth century, this particular call to God and its resultant practice of the monastic lifestyle became the meaning of *vocatio* (*God and the Common Life*, p. 18).

Reserved for professed "religious," vocation was no longer the domain of the ordinary Christian; indeed, the medieval Church held up the lives of clergy and religious as the ideal state, more pleasing to God than the lives of ordinary folk. It was this understanding of vocation that shaped religious thinking for centuries to come, and to some extent, continues to influence the thinking of many Christians today.

The monastic movement, however, affirmed and renewed a key insight into the nature of Christian vocation: the integration of the spiritual and material dimensions of life. For the monks, this insight was manifested by the necessity of regular prayer that unites the individual to both the community and to God. In the Benedictine tradition, this ongoing prayer of praise of the monks was named the Opus Dei or "the Work of God," and it was considered not only their chief work, but the place where God worked on them for their sanctification.

Following a daily pattern of communal singing and individual prayer, the Opus Dei joined the prayer of the particular community to the liturgical worship of the Church universal. At the same time, each monk was subject to the daily tasks he performed for the needs of the monastery. Taken together, the patterns of prayer and work formed a whole and healing life-rhythm that allowed each monk to become his best self—the self to which his Christian faith called him. It was this fulfillment of personal potential through the communal life that Benedict envisioned when he wrote his *Rule* in the early sixth century. As a miniature of the Church that integrated the call of the individual with the needs of the community and framed it with prayer, the Benedictine monastery modeled one image of the ideal Christian life.

Unfortunately, this was not a model that was available to the majority of the faithful who lived outside cloister walls. It would take almost a thousand years before Martin Luther challenged the Catholic Church's perspective on vocation.

The Call to Every Person

When Luther nailed his ninety-five theses to the door of Castle Church in Wittenberg in 1517, he launched a criticism of a multitude of Church teachings. Framed by his radical emphasis on Christian freedom and the integrity of the individual, Luther's theology demanded that the laity reclaim their participation in the work of the body of Christ on earth.

In opposition to the monastic and clerical ideals championed by the Church, Luther insisted that vocation belonged to every Christian, not just to those who chose to disavow the world. Relying on Scripture for his theological reflection, he turned to Paul's words (in 1 Corinthians 7:17) for the authority of his teaching: "let each of you lead the life that the Lord has assigned, to which God called you." In this passage,

Luther found the confirmation of his belief that earthly life and divine call belonged together, pronouncing that one's calling is not only to life here and now in the world, but that it is also intimately bound in the relationships of one's life. In addition to affirming the value of the inherent circumstances of one's life, it was equally important, Luther maintained, that all should remain in the state to which they were called.

According to Luther, every person occupies a "station," be it as spouse, child, parent, friend, employer, or employee. Because of the nature of the human condition, most people occupy multiple stations simultaneously. Each station carries with it great responsibilities as well as opportunities for "response-ability" as the individual interacts with others in the daily course of life.

If the station is lived out with love as God intends, the station is by its very essence helpful to others. "All stations," Luther preached, "are intended to serve others." This is vocation, the reformer taught—life in the earthly realm, directed not toward God, but toward one's neighbors. Yet God is certainly not excluded from Luther's formula. When the individual reaches out for others, God's creative work is carried on. It is in and through individual vocation that God's work of love takes form on earth (*Luther on Vocation*, p. 10).

This creative cooperation with God requires a great deal from each individual. Keeping in mind that one is not the cause of God's work, but only an instrument for it, demands a constant humility. In addition, since the individual has not chosen the vocation, but has been "assigned" it (along with its attendant relationships and obligations), Luther believed that struggle was inevitable. Doubts, loneliness, and despair can assail the Christian who feels inadequate to the tasks God has chosen for him or her. Combined with the realization that the individual's practice often falls short of God's intention, this self-appraisal can lead to the sense of vocation as a burden or, in Christian terms, as a cross.

Luther's solution is prayer and faith—belief that help from God is coming (though without preconceptions as to how God will act), and belief that one's vocation plays an integral role in God's plan for all creation. He writes in his *Annotationes*,

> Do not follow your own counsels and desires, but do what your hand finds before it. That is, continue in the definite work given to you and commanded by God, eschewing such things as would hinder you. Thus Samuel said to Saul, "You will be changed into a different man, and what your hand finds to do, do it." He did not prescribe a law to him, but whatever presented itself must be accepted and there is work to be done.

Following in Luther's footsteps, the French theologian John Calvin (who later moved to Switzerland) agreed with many of the theological insights of the German reformer. In particular, Calvin taught that it was the duty of all to serve as instruments of God on earth and in so doing, to become a part of the continuing process of creation. Like Luther, Calvin found equal dignity and value in all occupations and stations, affirming that individual work was the will of God. It is at this point, however, that Calvin's concept of the "elect" marks a significant departure from Luther's theology of vocation.

Whereas Luther believed all people were called by God to a holy life, Calvin was convinced that God had already chosen those people—the elect—who would receive eternal life. Everyone else, according to Calvin, was damned for all time, and there was nothing that could change that since God is unchanging. The elect, though favored by God, were nevertheless unidentified, leaving all to wonder about their eternal status.

In response to this unknowing, Calvin offered a means to the individual to ascertain one's probable fate. Since human work was the will of God, those who found success in their worldly occupations had evidence that they might expect inclusion in the elect. Consequently, the need to work and succeed in the material realm became a crucial task for Calvinists. Calvin considered it not only appropriate, but a religious imperative, for individuals to change occupations, if by doing so they could achieve greater financial earnings and thereby demonstrate their potential as one of God's elect. This allowance—even encouragement—to seek a change in one's work set a new precedent. Instead of being bound by the circumstances of one's life, the individual was given the mandate to exercise personal initiative in finding the situation that was most promising for accomplishing God's will.

By the end of the sixteenth century, a new understanding of vocation had evolved from a combination of Luther's and Calvin's theology. Work of all kinds was viewed as a calling for every person to serve God and no distinctions could be made that one occupation might be spiritually superior to another. In addition, material success was regarded as an indication of God's favor, so it behooved every person to work hard at an occupation to maximize profits and then reinvest those earnings so one's business might continue to grow, witnessing to the individual's obedience to God's will.

In 1904, Max Weber, the German economic sociologist, coined the term "Protestant ethic" for this new set of vocational beliefs. Today the term is "Protestant work ethic," and its key elements are still recognizably Calvinist: diligence, punctuality, gratification deferment, and the primacy of work. Now well-integrated into (or as some may argue, foundational to) the norms of Western culture, this ethic has lost much of its spiritual significance. For many people, it is completely severed from religious intention and interpretation.

The Call to Community

When Pope John XXIII convened the Second Vatican Council on October 11, 1962, he publicly announced his intention to metaphorically open the windows of the Roman Catholic Church and let a fresh wind blow through. In practice, he launched a recovery of the spirituality and vision of the earliest Christians—a spirituality that called everyone to holiness and community—that continues to this day. In the forty-plus years since Vatican II began its historic work, the Roman Church has struggled with many reforms, rejecting some and readily accepting others, while still influencing the shape of Christian thought around the world.

Perhaps the most dominant theological tenet to emerge from the work of the council has been its concept of the Church as the entire People of God, as stated in the document *Lumen Gentium*, the Dogmatic Constitution on the Church. By claiming that "all the faithful, scattered though they be throughout the world, are in communion with each other in the Holy Spirit" (no. 13), the document once again emphasizes the preeminent communal nature of the Christian faith. It insists that all members, through baptism, have a basic equality and common call to ministry (no. 33).

A second major thrust of Vatican II thinking can be found in *Apostolicam Actuositatem*, the Decree on the Apostolate of the Laity, which maintains that the People of God not only have a vocation, but that this vocation is by its very nature a vocation to the "apostolate"—a term meaning all activity that is directed to the goal of spreading the gospel throughout the world. In particular, this vocation of the laity carries a special responsibility for social outreach and the transformation of society.

Finally, in *Gaudium et Spes*, the Pastoral Constitution on the Church in the Modern World, the fathers of the council taught that Christians, particularly in the realm of work, must address "the more serious errors of our age,…the split between the faith which many profess and their daily lives.…Christians should rather rejoice that, following the example of Christ Who worked as an artisan they are free to give proper exercise of all their earthly activities and to their humane, domestic, professional, social, and technical enterprises…into one vital synthesis with religious values, under whose supreme direction all things are harmonized unto God's glory"(43). In this way, the Church urged members to actively seek and work toward the re-integration of faith and daily life. Such integration had seemingly slipped away in the wake of increasing contemporary industrialization and its accompanying compartmentalization of life experiences (*To Work and to Love*, p. 65).

Despite these landmark documents, the concept of vocation in the Catholic tradition continued to suffer from the distinction the Church maintained between lay and ordained persons. When the Church asked the People of God to pray for vocations, it referred to priestly and other ordained ministries, once again reserving "vocation" to only the vowed and ordained members of the community. Denied the permission to claim "vocation" for the fullness of their own callings, millions of Catholics were (and continue to be) unaware of the theological significance of what they do apart from Sunday worship.

In 1988, Pope John Paul II issued his apostolic exhortation *Christifideles Laici,* On the Vocation and the Mission of the Lay Faithful in the Church and in the World. Although this document also clearly distinguishes between lay and ordained members of the Catholic Church, it decrees that the lay faithful do indeed have a vocation that incorporates the multiple aspects of daily life. This call is not the sole arena of the ordained. "The call is addressed to everyone: lay people as well are personally called by the Lord, from whom they receive a mission on behalf of the Church and the world" (2).

Echoing the concern of *Gaudium et Spes,* the exhortation warns against the "temptation of legitimizing the unwarranted separation of faith from life, that is, a separation of the Gospel's acceptance from the actual living of the Gospel in various situations in the world" (2). At the same time, it applauds the "new manner of active collaboration" among the ordained and the laity, recognizing that only in community can the People of God come to a deeper awareness of the "gift and responsibility they share, both as a group and as individuals, in the communion and mission of the Church" (2).

In recent years, the Church has made aggressive efforts to educate its members about these important documents and their theological implications. The rapid growth of many grass-root ministries and community agencies within and outside the Roman Church seems to imply a new awareness of connectedness between individuals, their Christian identity, and their relationship to the larger community. Along with this development, great interest has been generated in exploring the emotional, religious, spiritual, and social aspects of what people do in their occupational roles. The growth in popularity of spiritual direction and personal coaching is one indication of this interest. No matter the means of address, however, the question of vocation revolves around a simple truth: it is about the way we live and why we live that way. For Christians, the answer is also simple: vocation is all about Christ.

CHAPTER 2

Anatomy

Paul carefully chose the metaphor of the body when he wrote about the Church as the body of Christ. Not only does a body describe an organic unity, but it allows for a diversity of parts and functions possessing their own integrity—an ideal model for fledgling Christian communities that were geographically isolated from each other and suffering spiritual growing pains. In addition, the metaphor of the body witnesses to the fundamental Christian belief of incarnation, spirit not only embodied, but integrated into the physical.

In the same way, the metaphor of the body is appropriate to vocation. It gives us an image of an integrated whole, composed of distinct, yet indispensable parts. By examining these parts—physical and spiritual alike—we can hope to understand not only their nature, but also how they interact and contribute to individual vocational development. In essence, we want to articulate the "anatomy" of vocation. Keeping in mind our goal of defining the theology of vocation, we will begin this task by sifting through the material of the preceding chapter to identify the basic building blocks of Christian vocation.

The Parts of the Body

Without question, "call" is the foundation of vocation. Beginning with Paul and up to the most recent documents issued by the Catholic Church, call is the starting point for any discussion of vocation. Indeed, as we have seen, Paul's original word *klesis*, or call, was the progenitor of the Latin *vocatio*, from which we have our English word *vocation*. Yet we have also seen that theological reflection, along with expanded interpretations of related Scripture passages, have broadened the concept of vocation beyond the call itself to include both personal and communal dimensions of the setting of the call and the effects of the call.

Call is the personal invitation from God to the individual to a purpose. In terms of our anatomy, we might name it the head and the heart of vocation. In Christian terms, it is a call to belief in Jesus Christ, which carries with it the inherent call to a community that shares that belief. God's call is uniquely tailored to every individual. As an invitation, it affirms the ability and freedom of each person to accept or reject God's communication. At the same time, it is clear that God is the one who initiates.

And God does so for a specific purpose. Throughout his writings, Paul was adamant that God's call to the individual was for the benefit of the community. In his first letter to the Corinthians, he explains that each Christian has a task to fulfill: "God has appointed in the church first apostles, second prophets, third teachers; then deeds of power, then gifts of healing, forms of assistance, forms of leadership, various kinds of tongues" (1 Cor 12:28). By claiming the individual's call—and gifts—for the needs of the community, Paul reveals an important insight into the theological nature of vocation: it is not "I" centered. The apostle insists, instead, that the individual's vocation takes its very shape, as well as its meaning, from the community it serves.

Luther elaborates on this key relationship between the outer and inner (or communal and personal) dimensions of vocation when he develops his understanding of stations (see page 11). Focusing on the outer realities of the individual's life—including personal and professional relationships, lifestyle, and the daily work one does—Luther builds a strong case for interpreting God's call to the individual in light of the given circumstances of one's life. Convinced that all life is holy, Luther sees significance in those particular circumstances as integral parts of the call issued by God.

In exercising responsibility for those circumstances, the individual is not only faithful to the call, but, according to Luther, participating in God's ongoing act of creation. In this way, Luther places vocation solidly in the realm of human experience, yet gives it a double meaning: vocation is both the situation of, and the individual's response to, God's call. Vocation, in a very real sense, connects the earthly reality of life with its supernatural dimensions.

Benedict likewise understood vocation as the individual's response in the world to God's call, although his world had the distinct qualification of being separated from the everyday existence of the general populace. Nevertheless, his contribution to a theological concept of vocation offers a significant foundation. Christian vocation, by integrating the material and spiritual worlds, brings the individual into the presence of God.

St. Paul's Transformation

Such integration is life-changing, which brings us to the second part of the anatomy of vocation: transformation. For 2000 years, Paul's conversion on the road to Damascus has been the archetype of the transformation effected by the response to call. (Since we are investigating vocation, we presume the individual's positive response to God's call; the failure to respond, or a negative response, is another study.)

Called personally by Christ, Paul was literally and figuratively brought to his knees and suffered blindness before his sight and health were restored upon his acceptance of that call. Made whole—physically and spiritually—by this surrender to Christ, Paul was transformed in both his spiritual life and his earthly vocation, rejecting his prior activity as a persecutor of Christians to become history's greatest evangelist. As he explains in his letter to the Philippians, he experienced a radical change of heart, counting all things as loss—which he had previously considered as gain. For those who likewise came to Christ, he decreed that their very existence had been fundamentally transformed. "There is no longer Jew or Greek, there is no longer slave or free, there is no longer male and female; for all of you are one in Christ Jesus" (Gal 3:28). Yet even this transformation pales before the ultimate one brought about by the resurrection of Christ. "You were dead through the trespasses and sins in which you once lived, following the course of this world," Paul writes in his letter to the Ephesians. "But God, who is rich in mercy, out of the great love with which he loved us even when we were dead through our trespasses, made us alive together with Christ" (Eph 2:1–2, 4–5).

Life from death can manifest itself in a multitude of forms. Luther, in examining the concrete details of daily life, taught that even an understanding of Christian vocation led an individual to a transformation of attitude toward the situation in which one already lived ("Luther on Vocation," p. 3). By recognizing one's relationships and responsibilities as part of God's design for the individual, the Christian's vision is directed to others, rather than remaining self-focused. This change in perspective can bring new energy and meaning into those interactions. Contemporary author Gregg Levoy maintains that calls announce a need for transformation in the individual and that the response that is engendered is an awakening of some kind (*Callings*, p. 2). This assertion echoes the scriptural command, "Sleeper, awake! Rise from the dead" (Eph 5:14).

In some cases, the transformation of vocation can produce saints, heroes, and martyrs, such as St. Augustine, Dietrich

Bonhoffer, Dorothy Day, and Archbishop Oscar Romero. In every case, transformation releases a spiritual power and a variety of gifts that the individual can draw upon to meet the demands of one's vocation. In our anatomy, we might imagine transformation as the body which carries vocation forward.

The "Hands" of Vocation

Theologically, gifts are given by God to an individual for a purpose. In terms of vocation, gifts are the instruments through which the individual acts. To use our body metaphor, gifts are the hands of vocation. This task-oriented nature of gifts is clear in Paul's letter to the Romans where he lists the gifts that Christians have to offer the community:

> We have gifts that differ according to the grace given to us: prophecy, in proportion to faith; ministry, in ministering; the teacher, in teaching; the exhorter, in exhortation; the giver, in generosity; the leader, in diligence; the compassionate, in cheerfulness. (Rom 12:6–8)

Paul's personal experience, however, reveals a key insight for an understanding of gifts in vocation in that it depicts a dynamic relationship between call, transformation, and gifts. Only after his conversion did Paul's true gifts become manifest and effective for God's purpose. Prior to his conversion, Paul was a zealous prosecutor. From his own admission, Paul was a man of conviction, intensity, and passion. In pursuit of Christians, these attributes served him well. In receiving his own call to Christ, these same attributes became the gifts God intended them to be in their unique historical significance.

Paul's experience yields three key insights into gifts: 1) though they may be present in some form (potential) in the individual prior to call/transformation, their fullest development occurs only in the context of realized vocation; 2) gifts are historically conditioned or dependent on the circumstances of the vocation; and 3) gifts are given to benefit both the person and the community. The implications of these insights are especially important when the individual is involved in discernment, whether it be the discernment of vocation or the discernment of the gifts themselves. We will return to these implications when we examine gifts in a later chapter.

The final component of vocation that emerges repeatedly from our historical review is community. Perhaps we can imagine it as the skin that covers the body to best represent its relationship to the other parts of vocation. It gives definition, shape, and cohesiveness to the vocation of the individual. As Paul, Benedict, Luther, Calvin, and contemporary theologians of all denominations have maintained, community is essential to the Christian's self-understanding. No one can be a Christian alone. Being Christian is rooted in an individual's identification with and moral formation by the community of believers.

From a theological perspective, the community is both the reason for and the ultimate beneficiary of the individual's vocation. "All stations are intended to serve others," Luther preached, confirming that personal vocation must be responsive to the relationships in which it is grounded. In a similar manner, Paul's discussions of gifts always focused on their contribution to the life of the community. "Let all things be done for building up," he teaches in 1 Corinthians 14:26. This building up, Paul insists, is the shared task and vocational goal of every Christian.

As a result of the community's preeminence, the personal dimension of vocation is subject to the communal. In practice, this dynamic admits, and sometimes demands, the sacrifice of the individual for the good of the community. In Christian language, this sacrifice is the way of the cross; it leads to suffering and, ultimately, to resurrection. At the same time, this subjection of the personal to the communal can be experienced by the individual as liberating. As theologian Dorothee Soelle describes it, "immersed in good work, our 'inborn egocentricity' vanishes, and in its wake the divine self within us is set free…good work releases the divine element in us by which we rediscover the source of our creativity and connection to all living things" (*To Work and To Love*, p. 96).

Theologically, then, joy and suffering are entwined in Christian vocation as the individual is repeatedly drawn beyond the limits of self-interest to embrace the community. In this self-transcendence, the community and the individual are renewed as "all of us, with unveiled faces, seeing the glory of the Lord as though reflected in a mirror, are being transformed into the same image from one degree of glory to another; for this comes from the Lord, the Spirit" (2 Cor 3:18).

The Example of Jesus

To validate our model of the anatomy of Christian vocation, we now turn to the example of Jesus (who is, in fact, the original source of all our vocational reflection). Using the gospel accounts as the evidence for our investigation, we will be limited to an exploration of what the authors recorded, remembering that these narratives are a mix of historical data, traditions of the earliest Christian communities, and reflections on the theological meaning of the life and death of Jesus. Despite these qualifications, the gospels still offer us fertile ground for study. Framed as biographies, they are good sources of the material as well as spiritual realities that inform the development of every human vocation, as well as the particular vocation of Jesus.

Though we cannot detail the where, when, and how of God's call to the historical Jesus, there are certain observations we can make: God's call to Jesus was individual, unique, historically conditioned, and purposeful, meeting all the criteria we have named in our vocational model. In the narratives of Jesus' baptism, we can readily identify two of these elements, most notably in God's announcement of a particular, unique relationship with Jesus: "This is my Son, the Beloved, with whom I am well pleased" (Mt 3:17). By taking the initiative in revealing this relationship, God makes an important statement: the source of Jesus' life and call is God.

As the story of Jesus unfolds, it is also clear that this call is not an egocentric enterprise designed for Jesus' self-gratification but rather a call to serve the community. As a result, Jesus' vocation takes its outer dimensions of direction and shape from the concrete needs of the community it serves in response to the surrounding circumstances. As a Jew of the early first century, there were historical conditions—such as Roman occupation, religious division, and oppressive social structures—with which he had to contend as he worked toward the fulfillment of his call. By locating the challenges of his call firmly in earthly relationships and circumstances, Jesus does not devalue or dismiss the material aspects of life, but instead models an awareness and appreciation of the complete human situation.

If we remain focused on just the historical aspect of the call of Jesus, however, we miss the spiritual dimension which not only definitively informs the work of Jesus but enlarges every vocation beyond the temporal. In Jesus' case, the integration of the material and spiritual, the human and the divine, is constitutive of his ministry as well as his being. Called by God to the task of redemption of the human community, Jesus attends to the spiritual health of the people by meeting them in the physical realities of their lives. In so doing, he breaks through the separation of the natural and supernatural worlds to reveal to others the presence of God. Following the head and heart of his call, Jesus acts as co-creator with God to fashion a new human situation: salvation.

Since we have no personal testimony from Jesus detailing his discernment of call and the private transformation he might have experienced as a result, we will consider the event of his baptism as the beginning of his vocational transformation. Like Paul, Jesus made public his acceptance of his call from God. Though we might speculate about any deliberations he might have made before taking the plunge into the Jordan, the New Testament record is silent in this respect. We do know that prior to his baptism, he worked as a carpenter. He surrendered this livelihood and its attendant lifestyle to do the new work given him by God.

According to the synoptic authors, the Holy Spirit was instrumental in this transformation. Matthew, Mark, and Luke all include in their narratives the vision of the Spirit descending upon Jesus, who was then led by that same Spirit to the desert. In the desert, Jesus submitted to a testing by the devil—a story that resonates with a rite of passage or transformation. Upon the completion of this testing, Jesus emerged from the desert a changed man. He returned to Galilee and began an active and powerful ministry of healing and preaching.

Here, too, we see the example of Jesus validating our model of vocation: in his transformation, Jesus accepts the call of God, surrenders what is necessary to fulfill that call, is made whole by that surrender (in Jesus' case, as proved by his successful contest against the devil), finds the circumstances of his life radically altered, and experiences the release of spiritual power and gifts.

Amazing Gifts

When Jesus begins his ministry in Galilee, he amazes the crowds with his gifts of wisdom, healing, and preaching. Again, the gospel record gives us no clues to Jesus' talents prior to his public appearance at the Jordan, save for Luke's narrative about Jesus as a young man conversing with the teachers in the temple in Jerusalem. Indeed, Luke's reference to Jesus who "increased in wisdom and in years, and in divine and human favor" (2:52) affirms to our vocational model that acknowledges the presence of (potential) gifts in the individual prior to transformation. Like Paul, Jesus' gifts became manifest and most effective in the service of his vocation.

The distinctive gifts of Jesus were perfectly matched to the requirements of his call, yet it is instructive to note that many of his visible gifts were common to others as well. Reports of healers, prophets, sages, and teachers abound in first-century literature, and recent scholarship has confirmed the existence of many individuals who performed what appeared (to their audiences) to be miracles. The key insight Jesus affords us is that his visible (and invisible) gifts are the gifts of God given for the benefit of the community, a purpose that bridged the human and divine. He spells this out for us in his comments upon hearing of the death of Lazarus, explaining that his ability to raise his friend from the dead is given so that the disciples might believe. Again and again, Jesus accomplishes the tasks God has set before him with the gifts he has been given—gifts that are practical and spiritual, powerful and particular.

Community is the reason, the setting, and the beneficiary of the vocation of Jesus. Early in his public ministry, Jesus made it clear that his purpose was to proclaim the gospel to the people of Israel. "The time is fulfilled, and the kingdom of God has come near; repent, and believe in the good news" (Mk 1:15). Motivated by this intent, all his actions were directed to that goal, whether it was preaching, healing, prayer, the gathering of disciples, teaching, the criticism of current religious or social practices, or turning over the money-changers' tables in the temple.

Despite the risks to his personal safety, Jesus continually chose to do his work for the good of the community, leading to a progression of personal sacrifices and suffering that culminated in his death on the cross. As our model has shown, and the example of Jesus confirms, the self-transcendence involved in sacrifice for the community results in two defining effects: personal transformation and communal renewal. In the case of Jesus, the ultimate effects were resurrection and the foundation of a community—a community grounded in the relationship between God and Christ that is the inheritance of all believers.

Judging from the comments of Jesus in several Scripture passages, he did not set out to create a new religion, but instead, to bring new life to the practice of the Jewish faith. "Do not think that I have come to abolish the law or the prophets; I have come not to abolish but to fulfill," he says in Matthew 5:17. In Luke's gospel, Jesus is portrayed as firmly grounded in the tradition of his people. His parents observed the laws of infant circumcision and purification. As a boy, he accompanied his family on the annual Passover pilgrimage to Jerusalem.

Throughout all the gospels, Jesus is depicted celebrating the traditional Jewish holidays and exhibiting the sensibilities of a first-century Jew, making it plain that his mission was to work within the community he knew. The fact that his life and death changed the very nature of the relationship between God and the entire human family—not just the Jewish people—was only understood by his disciples in the aftermath of his resurrection. Limited by their own religious and cultural perspectives, the companions of Jesus could not envision the full meaning of his vocation. Only as they themselves were transformed by the resurrection of Jesus and its effects, were they able, in turn, to more fully apprehend who Jesus was. Commissioned by Christ and empowered by the Holy Spirit, the disciples could then devote themselves to the transformation of the larger community.

A Clearer Understanding

By articulating an anatomy of vocation, we can come to a clearer understanding of vocation itself—what it consists of materially and spiritually, how those components interact and shape each other, how it works in the life of the individual, and its implications for ongoing personal and communal development. Crucial for our study are the theological insights yielded by this articulation. In the construction of our model and in the example of Jesus, we have uncovered important information about the relationship between our vocation, ourselves, and God, information that we can apply to deepen the meaning, as well as the experience, of our own vocations.

Chief among these insights is the recognition that vocation is the call of God that integrates the material and spiritual in the life of the individual. As a result, this call commands our attention, as it did in the example of Jesus, with an authority we cannot (or should not) deny. At the same time, this call affirms that we are in relationship with a God who wishes to include us in the ongoing work of creation. Our model also testifies that this call is a summons embedded not only in the concrete circumstances of our lives, but one that elicits our deepest authentic nature. Just as Jesus manifested his uniquely human and divine nature to accomplish his work, individuals access and develop their inner (and often, unknown) gifts in the course of realizing their vocations.

Personal transformation is the experience of the individual who answers God's call. While this transformation can occur in different ways and vary in intensity, our model indicates that it is precipitated or accompanied by surrender on the part of the individual— a surrender that effectively allows the individual to acknowledge the presence of God. For Paul, this surrender was dramatic and life-changing, resulting in a new self-identity. In his case, it was also a literal and figurative restoration to wholeness. This personal wholeness or sense of wellness is an important effect of the transformation that occurs in vocation, to which we will later return.

A final insight from our anatomy is that an individual vocation reaches beyond one's immediate community to affect broader and diverse groups. As Jesus' example demonstrates in the extreme, the accomplishment of his work extended beyond the community of the Jewish people to embrace all humanity. In similar ways, the vocations of individuals exert ripple effects that reach out to wider communities, sometimes creating startling connections and meanings, previously unimagined. Two theological implications are clear: 1) through our vocations, we cooperate in God's ongoing creative activity, and 2) to the extent we follow the vocational model of Jesus, we embody Christ in the world today. In the next chapters, we will examine ways we can enter more fully into our individual vocations by deepening our understanding of its different parts.

CHAPTER 3

Call

Call is the foundation of vocation. As Christians, we have already heard and responded to God's first call to us—the call to Christian community and identity. This call, however, is not the sole summons we receive from God in the course of our lives. Embedded in that first call are additional invitations from God to a specific purpose we have for the community. For some people, the invitations are clear and obvious. For many others, a particular call may be elusive, not fully formed or decipherable, requiring the individual either to exercise patience for the call to become clear or to seek assistance in understanding it. It is this call—which we have named the head and heart of vocation—that will provide our focus in this chapter as we examine the ways we hear, discern, and understand our own unique call of vocation.

A Case Study of Call

Oscar Romero was born in 1917 to a Roman Catholic family in the eastern portion of El Salvador. A quiet and studious boy, he longed to enter the seminary, which he did following an apprenticeship to a village carpenter. Ordained in Rome in 1942, Romero was immersed in doctoral studies when he was forced to leave the city in the midst of World War II. He returned to El Salvador and served in a series of assignments that included parish and diocesan work, a high school chaplaincy, and newspaper duties.

Conservative and cautious, Romero was concerned about the changes that the Second Vatican Council brought to the Church and troubled by the radical stance of the Latin American bishops who gathered in Columbia in 1968. Their alignment with the poor and oppressed who suffered from institutional and structural violence clashed with Romero's orthodox theology of peace and reconciliation, inviting consequences he was not prepared to accept. He believed (and as history would prove, rightly so) that the intention of the bishops to pursue social justice and liberation was to court conflict and division (*Oscar Romero*, p. 8). A supporter of the status quo, Romero also trusted in the basic goodness of those who held power in El Salvador. Even as late as 1974, when he was installed as bishop of Santiago de Maria, he believed that the escalation of violence against the poor was an aberration, not government policy.

It was during his tenure in Santiago de Maria that the quiet bishop began to really hear the cries of his impoverished flock, opening the rectory and other buildings to shelter those in need. As he ministered to the coffee plantation laborers and landless peasants who surrounded him, Romero began to see more clearly their helplessness against the will of the country's powerful elite. Deeply affected by their suffering, he privately condemned their unjust treatment at the hands of the wealthy landowners. His love for the poor, fed by his compassion and daily association with them in the often appalling circumstances of their lives, eventually led him to question his sympathies for the ruling oligarchy, though he made no public protest.

By the time Romero was made archbishop of San Salvador in 1977, the battle for land control had become a military-led orchestrated campaign of killings, torture, and violence against any peasant or priest who supported land reform. Despite the murder and torture of the people, however, Romero still hesitated to criticize the civilian authorities. A man of diplomacy and obedience, he valued the esteem of Rome and the other Salvadoran bishops who tacitly supported the status quo. Torn by his opposing loyalties to the poor and the bishops, Romero stood transfixed, unsure of his pastoral path.

Less than three weeks later, Oscar Romero heard the call of God when his good friend Rutilio Grande was murdered. Grande was a Salvadoran Jesuit who had worked tirelessly with the rural poor building Christian communities. Those who knew Romero insist that after the murder, Romero was never the same. "It was Rutilio's death that gave Archbishop Romero the strength for new activity," writes Salvadoran Jesuit Jon Sobrino, "and the fundamental direction for his own life" (*Archbishop Romero*, p. 5). Three years later, Romero, an outspoken, public archbishop who had unceasingly defended his people against the atrocities perpetrated by the military, was murdered as he celebrated Eucharist in a hospital chapel. Drawn beyond his own timidity, Romero had discovered the voice of God in the poor and oppressed. In so doing, he unleashed his vocational call as prophet and martyr.

We certainly are not all called to vocations as dramatically life changing or historically charged as Oscar Romero's. We can, however, learn much from it about the nature of vocational call and how it might function in our lives. As Romero's story illustrates, it is the fullness of vocational call—the call to the specific purpose God has intended in relation to the community—that is often difficult to hear. In Romero's case, a readiness to listen was critical, a readiness that resulted from years of training as a priest and pastor, as well as personal experiences that led to an awareness of and solidarity with the oppressed peasants and laborers. Romero's story also highlights a common characteristic of many calls: conflict. In his case, conflict was both an interior and exterior issue. As he grappled with his own developing understanding of the gospel, he was challenged to make changes in his practice of it. At the same time, he had to confront the external realities of his life that reflected the discrepancies between his conforming behavior and the demands of his emerging faith. Making sense of those conflicts and the call they carry is one of the aims of discernment, which we will consider later in this chapter.

Cultivating Silence

"Vocation does not come from willfulness," educator and author Parker Palmer writes in *Let Your Life Speak.* "It comes from listening." As Romero's life demonstrates and as Palmer goes on to explain, this particular type of listening is about cultivating silence that allows the individual to be attentive to (and sometimes surprised by) the inner truths and values of one's deepest authentic identity. For Romero, his listening drew him beyond his faithfulness to the status quo of the Church in El Salvador to pursue a justice that was intimately rooted in Jesus. His listening allowed him to dig deeper into Christian identity and find there new possibilities of hope, meaning, and response for himself and the people he served.

This type of listening requires readiness, discipline, and patience. Readiness is born of the accumulated events and circumstances of one's personal history. Discipline filters out distractions. Patience allows the call to unfold. For many people, it is also a formidable challenge because it requires them to make an honest appraisal of self-knowledge, or as Palmer puts it, "I must listen to my life." The difficulty in this, he points out, is that from our earliest years, we are taught to listen to others and not to ourselves. We are asked to conform to societal norms, expectations, and rules which may or may not accurately reflect our core values and truths. The result is that as we grow, the deepest parts of self are in danger of becoming lost or submerged in the layers of culture.

Seeking to reconnect with that original self, or listening to our life, is then a counter-cultural act. For every Christian, whose identity is grounded in the counter-cultural example of Jesus, this listening is both a challenge and a mandate of faith.

In *The Violence of Love*, Romero writes about the seductiveness of conformity and the courage it takes to move past it. "It is forgotten that mediocrity will always be majority and the courage of authenticity minority," he explains.

> Recall "the wide way" and "the narrow way" of the Gospel....In this difficult hour more than ever is there need for prayer, united with a genuine will to be converted, prayer that out of intimacy with God cuts one off from the confused clamor of life's shallow experiences, a will to be converted that is not afraid to lose prestige or privilege, or to change a way of thinking when it is seen that Christ insists on a new way of thinking that is more in keeping with his Gospel.

In Romero's experience, his listening drew him away from conformity to the dominant culture and closer to Christ as revealed in the poor. It also led him to solidarity with the oppressed. In that physical, emotional, and spiritual location, he was able to clearly hear his call of vocation.

It is at this point that Luther's theology of vocation—particularly his teaching about stations—can provide new insight into (and appreciation of) the relationship between our location and our call. To return to our case study, Romero had to firmly establish himself in the context of daily relationships with the poor in Santiago de Maria to be able to fully appreciate the reality of their lives. It was this reality that stirred his compassion and demanded a response. It was this response, which grew and matured in the course of his specific experiences, which culminated in his vocational fulfillment.

Without the people of Santiago de Maria, Romero's friendship with Rutilio Grande, and other significant relationships in his life, Romero might have been called to a different vocation. As Luther asserts, individual vocation is dependent upon and particularly suited to one's station (relationships with others). Conversely, one's stations are given by God. Christians who accept and recognize the gifts of the people in their lives as part of God's particular intention already are learning to listen for the call of vocation.

Cloaked in Conflict

Vocational calls are frequently cloaked in conflict. As noted earlier, Romero confronted conflict on several levels—personal, professional, religious, and social—each of which required him to examine his own self-understandings and how he lived them. Ultimately, he had to ask himself "Who am I?" (Or, as many contemporary theologians insist is the more accurate question, "Whose am I?") Changing the focus of the identity question from self to relationship carries with it profound implications for the individual, chief among them an almost seismic shift in understanding personal responsibility, power, and vulnerability.

The most immediate effect of this change in the question is that it identifies the individual through connection to others, placing a primacy on relationship and not on the independent self. Identity is about bonds. In Christian terms, it is the individual's life in communion with the Body of Christ. This identification is also consistent with our theology of Christian vocation, which names vocation as the purpose one is called to serve for the community. By identifying oneself in terms of the community first, vocation is then a natural response—and responsibility—to others. In claiming an identity based on community, the Christian facilitates the transcendence of the communal, thereby radically altering the individual's priorities and actions.

Likewise, issues of power and vulnerability look different through the lens of the "Whose am I?" question. Power is not a personal possession, but issues from the community. In his 1979 pastoral letter, Romero relied on this understanding of power to argue that the Church's mission is to be "an empowerer" as the agent of God. In order to do this, presence is critical. "This demands of the Church a greater presence among the poor," he wrote. "It ought to be in solidarity with them, running the risks they run, enduring the persecution that is their fate...." By calling for the Church's power to be vested in the vulnerable, Romero reveals a startling truth that many individuals prefer to ignore: when vulnerability is shared in community, it produces power. Seen in this light, vulnerability is a gift that builds up the community rather than a liability that tears it down. On the personal level, "Whose am I?" also transforms vulnerability into strength. Rather than exposing weakness, vulnerability is the means by which the individual is drawn into closer relationship with others.

When individuals make the identity leap from self to relationship, and experience the attendant transformation of perspective, it affects vocational call in three ways: it causes conflict, demands resolution, and prepares the individual to hear the call of vocation. In Romero's case, all three effects were present. His personal self-examination, reflection, prayer, and courage to confront conflict remain solid models of example for every individual preparing to answer the call of Christian vocation.

A final observation about conflict and call needs to be made. Just as call may be cloaked in conflict, conflict may be the call itself. For Romero, this seemed to be true. His vocation unfolded as he embraced the struggle of the people and made it his own. For many Christians, however, conflict may simply serve as the flag that draws attention to the call waiting to be heard.

The task for the individual, then, is to sort out what the conflict is pointing toward and to try to make sense of the vocational call behind it. In some cases, we may even be tempted to dismiss the call itself because of its outer wrappings. As Palmer puts it, the call "may come from the wrong place or for the wrong reason, but that does not mean that it is the wrong call" (*The Active Life*, p. 59). For those struggling with the task of identifying a call, discernment is a necessary part of the process.

The Art of Discernment

Discernment is a traditional tool used by Christians throughout the ages to assist them in listening to and understanding the call of vocation. By drawing on the intuitive, intellectual, emotional, and rational resources of the individual (and in some cases, the community), discernment is a process that attempts to creatively listen to, interpret, and integrate different types of information about the individual and/or the situation in order to find direction for one's action. Some scholars have referred to discernment as the art of listening to the head and the heart, while others say it is about the leadings of the Holy Spirit and wisdom.

In a narrow sense, discernment is a specific process of deliberating and testing specific options. In a broader sense, it is the "discernment of spirits," a habit and gift of wisdom that listens to all the voices in experience to find the invitation and presence of God. (*Go and Do Likewise*, p. 152)

In the practice of Quakers, discernment is about clarity found through community. When a Quaker is unsure of a call, select members of the community are gathered as a "clearness committee" to help the individual sort out the issues. Their method is not confrontational or prescriptive. They ask questions, inviting the individual to seek and reflect on the answers that emerge from within. Relying on the Spirit living in every person, the committee provides space and quiet for that Spirit to speak, while affirming the values of self-knowledge and communal support in the process of hearing a call.

An unstructured type of communal discernment is the insight provided by friends and acquaintances in informal settings. Many people frequently experience this type of discernment without realizing its value. Comments and observations casually offered by friends may contain truths that are often overlooked. Romero gained direction and inspiration not only from his association with the dispossessed but also from their personal remarks to him. Such remarks brought him new understanding about his abilities and pastoral responsibilities. In his diary, Romero often referred to the guidance and clarity he gained from those he met. In commenting on his meeting with the Commission of Laity, he wrote, "The group has goodwill and I believe being able to reflect with them about such a crucial section of the Church, the laity, I will be enriched by their judgments" (*The Violence of Love*, p. 56).

In a similar way, compliments or questions raised by a friend might unveil personal interests or strengths of which one is unaware, thereby providing an impetus to consider and explore new avenues of self-expression or realization. Remarks like "You are so good with teenagers" or "Have you ever thought about being an artist?" or "You can think things through so clearly" may be springboards to calls that have lain hidden, dormant, or even previously rejected. Whatever form it takes, discernment that flows from the community—be it deliberate or unconscious—can be a fertile source of self-understanding in preparation for hearing vocational call.

Mentoring is another approach to discernment that has a long history in the Christian tradition. Honored as a relationship of learning by the ancient Greeks, Christian mentoring brings together two individuals, one of whom acts as guide or teacher for the other in personal formation. In his study of mentoring, Edward Sellner maintains that in its most fundamental sense, mentoring is about transformation. The mentor helps the mentee encounter the larger self that is maturing within. In the case of spiritual mentoring, it is "a form of empowerment that helps others discern their vocations, acknowledge their gifts, and begin to give shape to their dreams" (*Mentoring*, p. 59). In this effort of self-knowledge, the mentor assists the individual by encouraging attentive listening to those dreams and seeking ways to bring them to fruition. In recent years many people have rediscovered the value of mentoring in the form of spiritual direction and found it to be extremely helpful in identifying potential pathways for vocational direction.

Perhaps the most common and most elemental type of Christian discernment is personal prayer. Romero, a man known for his devotion to regular solitary times of prayer, believed that prayer has the power to lift the individual beyond the "confused clamor of life's shallow experiences," allowing one to see more clearly God's priorities. Jesus, of course, is the model of Christian prayer. In the gospels he is often depicted as seeking and devoting himself to private prayer, making it plain that prayer not only sustains him in his ministry but also provides clarity for his work. In the Garden of Gethsemane, he uses words that every Christian may echo in a prayer for discernment: "Not my will but yours be done" (Lk 22:42). Through prayer, the Christian seeks union with the mind of God in order to better understand the call of vocation "not according to our works but according to his own purpose and grace" (2 Tim 1:9).

A Complex Process

By looking at Oscar Romero's personal experience, we find ample evidence of the complexity involved in vocational call. As the foundation of vocation, call is the starting point for every Christian who seeks to make manifest God's particular purpose in life. Unfortunately, the call of vocation for the individual is not always presented in precise language. More often than not, it is embedded in the circumstances of one's life and requires personal effort to uncover it. Simply hearing the call requires a readiness that is the product of personal experience, patience, and attentiveness to surrounding circumstances and relationships.

Many times, call is experienced as conflict, with self or with others. In the course of resolving these conflicts, the individual may be challenged to rigorous self-examination and radical self-exploration, which may result in a new openness to the call itself.

Finally, in the effort to make sense of the call, discernment is a traditional approach that cultivates and integrates insights from both the individual and the community. As it deepens the Christian's understanding of call, it also generates new opportunities and demands for individual transformation.

CHAPTER 4

Transformation

In our anatomy analogy, transformation is the body that carries and moves vocation forward. Responding to call, the individual experiences a transition or change that may express itself in a variety of ways and produce an array of effects.

Whereas conversion refers to a change of heart, vocational transformation is the means by which one is equipped to meet the demands of a specific call. For some, this transformation might involve concrete changes in circumstances, social or physical location, or jobs. For others, it might be a completely interior experience that radically alters how one perceives and interacts with the ongoing realities of life. In some cases, transformation may appear to be triggered by a specific event. As we saw in the last chapter, the friends of Oscar Romero believed the murder of Rotilio Grande was the catalyst behind the archbishop's active and very visible involvement in the cause of the peasants. In other people's experience, transformation may be a gradual process that takes months or even years to fully manifest its effects. For some, there may not be any awareness of change, and it is only in retrospect that the transformation is obvious.

Despite the differences among individual experiences, there are five characteristics that seem to be consistent with vocational transformation: timing, surrender, breakthrough, freedom, and empowerment.

A Case Study of Transformation

Clare Offreduccio (St. Clare of Assisi) was born around 1193 into a family of wealth and privilege in the prosperous town of Assisi in an era of political and economic upheaval. Within a few years, the threat of escalating violence compelled Clare's father to send his wife and children into exile across the valley to the town of Perugia. There, Clare lived quietly with her mother, Ortulana, her two sisters, and several kinswomen for four years.

When the women returned, Assisi was awash with change. The new merchant class and the feudal lords had assembled a fragile peace that allowed them to live together and rebuild the city, which was now an independent, self-proclaimed "commune." Following her mother's example, Clare gave alms and food to the poor. As one of her oldest friends testified for her canonization process, Clare was, from her youth, "intent upon and occupied with works of piety" (*Clare of Assisi*, p. 129).

It was Clare's association with Francis of Assisi, however, that has dominated history's remembrance of her. After hearing Francis preach and meeting him several times in secret, Clare determined to follow the footsteps of Jesus that Francis had revealed to her. In defiance of her father and conventional expectations of marriage or monastery, Clare left her family in the middle of the night and consecrated herself to God, choosing to live a life of obedience, poverty, and chastity. As a visible sign of her consecration and its inherent transformation of her life, Francis cut her hair. Her infuriated father tried to bring her home by force. She resisted and clung to her choice until he abandoned his attempts.

When Clare was quickly joined in her vows by other women, Francis prevailed upon her to accept the responsibility and office of abbess for the newly-forming community. In the years to come, she gave herself fully to that task, always mindful of the example she gave of humility, service, and love for Christ. In the process, she became a powerful model of devotion and leadership for Christians everywhere. Not only did she lay the foundation for her own order of the Poor Clares, but she was the confidante and spiritual adviser to popes, princesses, and other members of the Franciscan family.

Through the *Rule* she wrote for her community, Clare left a lasting vision for the imitation of Christ that had called her to surrender herself to God when she was only eighteen. In challenging the Church and society's expectations of her day, she broke through the traditional structures that limited women's practice and expression of faith, granting them a freedom they had previously been denied in religious life. In so doing, she blazed a trail for generations of women to follow in their search for authentic spirituality.

Clare's life provides ample material for exploring the nature and function of vocational transformation. By combining these observations with the insights of both classic and contemporary theologians, we can draw some key conclusions about transformation that will help each of us recognize and understand its effects in our own lives.

We will now consider five components that effectively describe the dynamics of transformation, as mentioned before, in the context of Clare's story.

The Right Time

When Clare heard the preaching of Francis, she recognized her call to her personal vocation. A devout Christian, she had already secretly vowed herself to celibacy. She did so, knowing her father would not accept her decision because her marriage would enhance the family's fortunes. Locked in a battle of wills with her family, the invitation of Francis' teaching offered her the route she was seeking to join herself to God. By seizing the moment of opportunity Francis presented, Clare was able to set in motion her response to God and begin her vocational development.

In Luther's theology, this concept of opportunity was named "the hour" and he believed it was critical to understanding vocation. Rather than pinning it to one specific incident in the life of the individual, however, he taught that "the time" was a product of God's work in the world. This work shapes situations and relationships that surround the person and offer potential for response. Viewed from this perspective, "the hour" is God's intentional gift to the individual that allows the Christian to enter into vocation—a gift that encompasses past and present.

In Clare's case, this double meaning of "the hour," as a specific present opportunity and as the accumulation of experience, seems accurate. Certainly her unique reaction to Francis was dependent on her history. Luther's inclusion of potential response also incorporates the element of future time in his theology of vocation. As he expressed it, when "the hour" arrives, the individual, through his or her actions, is a coworker with God, one who is actually participating in God's creative action. Seen in terms of Clare's ongoing transformation from defiant daughter to revered abbess, "the hour" spanned her vowed life, continually challenging her to grow into the vocation to which God had called her.

Willing Surrender

Timing alone is not enough to propel the individual into vocational transformation. No matter how much Clare's past had prepared her for Francis, it still required her act of will to leave her family and leap into an unknown future. Called by God, she knowingly surrendered, making herself vulnerable and exposed to the reactions of others. Aware of the complications and anger she would bring upon herself, Clare was undeterred in her decision. Seen in this context, Clare's surrender was an intimate act of personal strength that combined with "the hour" of her call to effect her transformation.

It is important to our model of vocation to clarify this understanding of surrender as strength and not weakness. In contemporary culture, surrender is typically perceived as a negative value, giving up of privilege, possessions, or power in the face of another's demands or threats of consequence. When most people speak of surrender, they focus on the diminishment of the individual, interpreting it as an unattractive submission that acknowledges powerlessness. In each of these instances, surrender is limiting and seen primarily as a response, not an initiative of the individual.

What we see in the surrender to vocation is significantly different. As Clare's example demonstrates, it is an act of will that is grounded not in weakness but in strength—in particular, the strength of faith. By surrendering to God's call to a vocation that was, at the time, non-existent in its shape, Clare drew on her personal power to hand that same power over to God. Clare did have other options. Had virginity alone been her goal she could have joined a comfortable convent of the Benedictines, who retained personal property and material assets (*The Call of St. Clare*, p. 33). Yet her call was to something more. To find out what it was, she needed to place herself completely in the hands of God.

Contemporary writer Gregg Levoy states this in another way. Surrender involves giving up the transitory for the sake of the transcendent. He says that surrender poses this question: "What are you willing to give up to ensure your own unfolding, and the unfolding of what is holy in your life?" (*Callings*, p. 11). Clare's deliberate surrender of her whole life was her answer to that question. She chose not out of desperation, but out of trust and love. Seen from this perspective, surrender is a positive value in the development of Christian vocation, reversing the conventional concept of surrender as negative. Paul's words from 1 Corinthians 1:25 come to mind: "God's foolishness is wiser than human wisdom, and God's weakness is stronger than human strength."

A final observation about Clare's surrender is necessary. Rather than limiting her potential, her surrender removed the limits that constrained her in her pursuit of her vocation. In this way, she was able to surpass the barriers that obstructed her, an act that simultaneously made her both vulnerable and powerful. It is this breakthrough experience to which we now turn as the central component of vocational transformation.

The Importance of Breakthrough

As Clare's case illustrates, vocational breakthrough results from the radical combination of two opposing forces: vulnerability and strength. In her study of the passionate nature of God, theologian Rosemary Haughton fastens on this dynamic as the predictor of personal transformation.

> Each breakthrough in human life releases the person into a new sphere of his or her own personality, but also into a capacity for deeper communion with others. The extent, and therefore the power, of the potential thus made available depends on two things: greatness of the need to break through and the willingness to "be broken." (*The Passionate God*, p. 82)

Certainly, the action of this dynamic manifested itself powerfully in Clare's life, enabling her to divest herself of the personal security of what she knew, to seek a vocation she only could sense. If we are to be thorough in our investigation of breakthrough, however, we must look deeper into Clare's experience and attempt to identify the very impulse that produced her breakthrough experience. Using Haughton's theology of the nature of God, that impulse is love, and its operation is passion.

Haughton proposes that passion is a template for understanding the way God loves people. She suggests that by looking at the way people love people and in particular at the love we call "passionate," we can learn things about how love operates that we might not otherwise discover.

We can say "love" and mean a restful, gentle, and essentially kind experience. But if we say "passion," we evoke something in motion—strong, wanting, needy, concentrated toward a very deep encounter. It is a violent word. Yet it has, in its roots, obviously a "passive" sense. "Passion" also implies a certain helplessness, a suffering and undergoing for the sake of what is desired and, implicitly, the possibility of a tragic outcome. (p. 7)

Clearly, Clare loved God in this way as she surrendered to God's call. Focused on following Jesus, she was simultaneously active and passive, strong and vulnerable. Her concentration of love was definitely aimed at moving her into a life-changing encounter with God, and at the hour of her surrender, this passionate love leapt the gap between what was her life and what it would become. In Haughton's language, passion is the leap of faith, a "timeless instant of oneness," an "experience of recognition so complete and profound that it's impossible to say what is recognized."

Yet it is not a leap fostered in sentimentality or emotionality, though great emotion may be released by it. Clare's story verifies this. Well aware of the material, social, and familial repercussions of her leap of faith, Clare nonetheless made it, and as a result she bore not only a storm of emotion from her father but from herself as well. Painful though she found it to be, her breakthrough of passion thrust her into a new world, a world that offered her the freedom to explore that "new sphere of her own personality," as Haughton describes it. In psychological and spiritual terms, Clare's breakthrough might also be characterized as a movement toward wholeness or the opportunity to discover her deepest personal truths—a process she could have initiated only in passionate response to God's call to her.

The communal dimension of passionate breakthrough must also be noted. In Clare's example, her actions sent ripples—even waves—of reaction through her family and the larger community of Assisi. Not long after her father's failed attempt to regain her,

Clare's sister followed her into poverty, as did increasing numbers of women in the area. Transformed by her breakthrough, Clare developed a great capacity for a deeper communion with others, as Haughton claims. This capacity, while personal, served her growing community of sisters as well as the numerous people with whom she corresponded and counseled in spiritual matters. Keeping in mind our thesis that Christian vocation is given to the individual for the purpose of serving the community, we can now observe that the breakthrough of transformation itself fulfills the same purpose.

The arena of the breakthrough of vocation is not the sole domain of the human person or community, however. As Luther was careful to explain in his theology of vocation, Christians are living instruments in the hand of the creating God, the point where something more breaks into the world (*Luther on Vocation,* p. 233). Using this model, we can view the vocational breakthrough of the individual from the divine perspective. Through Christian transformation, God finds new outlets and opportunity for creation, effectively making all vocation a participation in God's creative work. By combining Luther's and Haughton's models, perhaps a fuller understanding of Christian vocational breakthrough can be articulated. Propelled by mutual passion, God and the individual act cooperatively to break through what already exists to allow for the creation of something new.

In order to accomplish this, God acts both with and on the individual through the vehicle of transformation. Subject only to God's intention, the duration of breakthrough and its effects are variable. It can be an isolated incident that marks a distinct change in the individual or it can be a continuing process of transformation. In Clare's story, both types of breakthrough are evident in her consecration at the hands of Francis and her lifelong development as abbess of her order. Yet these differing experiences of breakthrough produced the same effects: freedom and empowerment.

Freedom and Empowerment

As barriers fall to breakthrough, the individual emerges with a newfound sense of freedom. New horizons replace old ones while attitudes and understandings of present situations or circumstances are transformed by the energy released as a result of breakthrough. Frequently these changes are primarily internal for the individual. External realities also can be altered as a result of individual breakthrough.

Without a doubt, Clare's physical and social circumstances changed when she left her family's home, providing her with a personal sense of release that was tempered by her recognition of trials ahead. At the same time, her freedom fed her determination to hold fast to her chosen path, and she did not waver in her defiance of her father. Nor did her strength of vision or commitment to her community falter in her later years. Secure in her faith, she untiringly defended her order's "privilege" of poverty despite the efforts of bishops and popes to wrest it from her. She once confided in a letter to Agnes of Prague, "If anyone would tell you something else or suggest something which would hinder our perfection or seem contrary to our divine vocation, even though you must respect him, do not follow his counsel" (*Francis and Clare*, p. 197). A woman grown wise in the continual transformation of her vocation, Clare did not hesitate to use the freedom she won at great cost as a young woman. Holding herself responsible to her community members, she modeled for them collaborative leadership that acknowledged the personal integrity—and power—of every individual.

Luther's reflections on vocational transformation might be well applied to Clare's example, while offering insight into the experience of every individual. When Christians truly know they are acting under divine command in performing work, they experience an unexpected power from that work, Luther maintained. In particular, when one is acting in concert with "the hour," everything one does seems to proceed almost effortlessly. In this way, following one's vocation is liberating and empowering. Perhaps the most visible manifestation of that empowerment can be found in the gifts of the individual who has experienced vocational transformation.

CHAPTER 5

Gifts

An appreciation of one's abilities, aptitudes, skills, talents, and inclinations as gifts grows out of the Christian understanding of personal relationship with God. Created by a loving God, the individual has been endowed with particular gifts according to the intention of God. These gifts, moreover, carry a mandate with them. Since "we have gifts that differ according to the grace given to us" (Rom 12:6), let us exercise them. Gifts have a purpose for both the individual and the larger community. In our anatomy, we have named gifts as the hands of vocation, the means whereby we address and perform the specific tasks of our individual call. As we read in the last chapter, transformation is the agent that empowers the gifts of vocation by releasing those that are restrained and revealing those that have been hidden.

A Case Study of Gifts

Clive Staples Lewis was born in 1898 in Belfast, Northern Ireland. An imaginative boy, he and his older brother, Warren, spent hours together telling stories and playing them out in their childhood home, creating whole worlds and complete histories of fantasy with toy figures and models. When his mother died in 1908, Lewis continued to find comfort and company in his imaginative life and in books. As a student in boarding schools, he indulged his passion for literature and devoted himself to reading the classics, finding himself especially drawn to the great romances and mythic legends. Raised as a Christian, he rejected the faith in his early teen years and embraced atheistic intellectualism instead.

He was a student at University College in Oxford in 1917 when World War I erupted in Europe. Leaving his studies, he enlisted in the British army and was sent to France, where he was wounded in 1918 and subsequently returned to England. By 1925, he was a Fellow of Magdalen College in Oxford, working as a tutor in English language and literature, writing papers, and enjoying the academic life. Yet he felt a compulsion that led him to search for something more. After years of reflection marked by his own intellectual resistance and ongoing study with friends, Lewis finally surrendered to the spiritual pull he experienced and made the "absolute leap in the dark," as he described it in his autobiography *Surprised by Joy*. He admitted that God was God, and he knelt and prayed. Two years later, he became a Christian.

In the years that followed, his writing took on new dimensions as he continued to teach at Oxford and later at Cambridge. His personal secretary, Walter Hooper, believed that Lewis "could write no great works until he was converted to Christianity…after which he ceased to take much interest in himself" (*The Weight of Glory*, p. 2).

Lewis focused on writing the works that made him one of the most popular and enduring Christian authors of modern times. His *Chronicles of Narnia*, science fiction novels, theological and spiritual works were among the more than thirty books he wrote, allowing him to reach a broad audience, crossing both age and denominational differences. In addition, Lewis corresponded with thousands of people, offering encouragement, advice, and personal wisdom, believing that his letter writing was both an act of Christian humility and an opportunity for the Holy Spirit to work through him. The vocational development that most surprised Lewis, however, was his preaching.

According to one friend, Lewis would never have imagined his career would take him in that direction, noting that "Lewis often said that if anyone had told him in his atheist days that he would someday step into a pulpit and preach, he would have considered that man raving mad" (*Mentoring*, p. 46). Yet the years leading up to World War II found him in various chapels delivering sermons, and in 1941, at the invitation of the British Broadcasting Company, he began to give live radio talks about Christianity. A dynamic speaker, Lewis had a unique gift for connecting with his audiences and conveying the power of his convictions and personal witness. Insistent that he was a "mere Christian," Lewis influenced and inspired generations of people with both his spoken and written words.

Since every person's particular gifts vary, our intention in this chapter is not to create a catalog of all possible skills or abilities but rather to understand in broad strokes how gifts appear and function in vocation, so that the individual can apply this knowledge to her or his own experience. By studying Lewis' life, we can draw some conclusions about the nature, discernment, and development of vocational gifts. Using examples from his experience, important patterns emerge that help inform both the vocation-seeker and our theological model of vocation. In addition, we can now take a closer look at the three key insights proposed in Chapter Two by tracing their implications in the concrete details of Lewis' life.

The Nature of Gifts

Though gifts may be present in some form (potential) in the individual prior to call/transformation, their fullest development as gift only occurs in the context of realized vocation.

In his autobiography, Lewis writes affectionately and at length of his youthful imaginative play and love of stories. As an adult, he was able to draw on those childhood passions as both a teacher and a writer, producing the greatest body of his work after he found his vocation as a Christian author. This relationship between the passions of youth and adult vocation is one that demands attention for many reasons. It can offer vocational direction, assist in the discernment of vocational gifts, revive dormant gifts, restore a sense of purpose for the individual, and reveal an integration or wholeness in the individual.

For Lewis, his childhood passions were clear indicators of his adult vocational direction. Throughout his life he never turned away from his imaginative gifts and the desire to tell stories. The joy he found in those passions sustained him in the difficult periods of his life, giving him both a sense of direction and personal purpose in his work. Lewis was fortunate to find, recognize, and nurture his gifts at an early age. Perhaps we might call him doubly blessed in that he enjoyed his gifts, but also had the self-knowledge and confidence to keep nurturing and developing them—despite what others might have thought about their real-world value. In this respect, Lewis teaches an important truth about the nature of gifts: they must be accepted and embraced as personally meaningful in order for them to grow and flourish.

This embrace, however, does not necessarily come easily or naturally to every person. For any number of psychological, emotional, intellectual, or social reasons, many individuals reject their innate gifts to focus their energies on what they (or the culture) deem to be more desirable, useful, or marketable attributes. It is in opposition to this attitude that the counter-cultural stance of Christian vocation once again becomes evident.

Christian vocation is commissioned by God, not by human dictates. As a result, the intention of vocations and the means by which individuals are to fulfill those vocations cannot be measured or appraised by human standards. Instead, it is the Christian's responsibility to be open to the gifts God gives and to the possibilities those gifts may present for personal growth and communal benefit. In *The Active Life*, Palmer expounds on this responsibility.

Every human being is born with some sort of gift, an inclination or an instinct that can become a full-blown mastery. We may not see our gift for what it is. Having seen it we may choose not to accept the gift and its consequences for our lives. Or, having claimed our gift, we may not be willing to do the hard work necessary to nurture it. But none of these evasions can alter the fact that the gift is ours. Each of us is a master at something, and part of becoming fully alive is to discover and develop our birthright competence.

Embracing that birthright is essential for the individual's experience of being "fully alive," as Palmer calls it. In theological terms, we might conclude that the nature of God's vocational gifts to the individual is, in reality, twofold: 1) to provide the means by which the Christian can serve the community, and 2) to provide a means whereby the individual can experience personal wholeness.

The fact that the keys to this personal wholeness lay in childhood passions comes as no surprise to those who study child psychology. Young children do not judge their natural gifts—they explore them. As psychologist Jean Piaget explained it, the cognitive development of the person involves a process of transformation of thought in the direction of greater internal differentiation and complexity. It is the task of the person at each stage of cognitive development to assimilate what is known in the environment into existing structures of thought (*Stages of Faith*, p. 49). Not yet having developed sophisticated discriminatory thought processes, young children readily welcome and experiment with the talents and interests they find emerging in themselves. Unfettered by adult rationalizations and critiques, children are uniquely suited to try out the raw gifts with which God has endowed them.

Over time, those gifts with particular attraction for the child can grow into passions and assume special meaning for the developing individual. Writer and poet David Whyte names these same childhood experiences as powerful precursors of both adult wholeness and vocational direction.

> Whatever particular horizons drew us as a child are the original patterns and templates of our adult belonging. They are clues as to how we find our measure of happiness and satisfaction in the world. (*Crossing the Unknown Sea*, p. 68)

Jesus, too, affirmed the value and importance of childhood openness when he said, "Truly I tell you, whoever does not receive the kingdom of God as a little child will never enter it" (Lk 18:17). The challenge for every individual, then, is to use those childhood clues and that childlike trust to discover one's unique gifts of vocation.

The Discernment of Gifts

Gifts are historically conditioned or dependent on the circumstances of the vocation. Uncritical openness is crucial for allowing our gifts to emerge and also necessary for discerning the vocational import of particular gifts. Thanks to his unabashed love for storytelling, C.S. Lewis was able to give free rein to the development of his creative imagination, unaware that the gift would take on new dimensions and significance in his later work as a Christian writer and speaker. By remaining open to the possibilities and opportunities he encountered in his experience, Lewis found new meaning and power in the gifts he was already using.

The role of opportunity in the discernment of gifts was not lost on Luther. "Do what your hand finds before it" was his repeated exhortation in his *Annotationes*. "Always pursue that which is present to your hands and belongs to your vocation." Judging from his life story, Lewis followed a similar directive, exploring all types of options, such as teaching, writing, and speaking, that arose in the course of his work. Yet even Lewis himself could not have anticipated that the full unfolding of his talents would include a turn at preaching. In his case, it seems clear that the actual historical circumstances in which he found himself, World War II, exerted a calling forth of previously hidden gifts.

Lewis' experience leads to another observation about the discernment of gifts. The individual can be unaware of personal gifts that are evident to others. In Lewis' case, his potential as a preacher was recognized and encouraged by Canon T.R. Milford, a vicar who admired Lewis' writing and invited him to deliver a sermon in his church. In many ways, Lewis returned the favor in his prolific personal correspondence, often offering words of encouragement and discernment to those he wrote and helping them name gifts they might otherwise have missed. As mentor and friend, he was both sounding board and guide to those who relied on his Christian perspective.

Palmer, in his work with small groups, frequently directs people to help each other identify the gifts they use in specific situations, pointing out that it is an "affirming experience to see our gifts at work in a real-life situation—and it often takes the eyes of others to help us see." The reason those gifts can be difficult to discern is because the individual is too close to them. As Palmer explains it in *Let Your Life Speak*, our strongest gifts are frequently those we do not realize we possess.

> They are a part of our God-given nature with us from the moment we drew first breath, and we are no more conscious of having them than we are of breathing. (p. 52)

Gaining others' perspectives on one's own natural abilities, seeking new opportunities, following inclinations and interests, and remembering childhood passions all can be paths to identifying and embracing personal gifts. Placed in the context of one's personal history and present circumstances, those same gifts can take on even greater significance and power as they are interpreted in the light of Christian vocation.

The Development of Gifts

Gifts are given to benefit both the person and the community. Though the discernment of one's gifts can often be a result of community involvement, it remains the responsibility of the individual to develop those gifts. John Calvin believed it was every Christian's duty to find the best use of one's gifts in order to accomplish God's purpose. Unlike Luther, who insisted that the individual remain in the situation in which he found himself, Calvin demanded that Christians aggressively seek the best use of gifts, even if it required disruptive change. Either way, the development of gifts is a process that once initiated benefits both the individual and the community as those gifts are brought to fruition and put to work in service to others.

Dorothee Soelle emphasizes that using one's gifts is a path to self-discovery. By engaging our gifts in good work, "we discover who we are, we assume responsibility for ourselves and others, and we lay the foundations for our own future and society's future" (*To Work and To Love*, p. 89). No matter one's endeavor—working as a tradesperson, corporate executive, or parent—consciously and conscientiously doing good work gives the individual the opportunity to utilize and develop gifts.

As self-expression, work allows the individual to grow into a full realization of personal identity. Using Lewis' experience as an example, the vocation-seeking Christian can draw on natural gifts and personal passions to find work that resonates with one's deepest self. It is, however, the development of these gifts as they are used that brings the individual wholeness. Soelle sees this dynamic of gift development as a clear connection of the individual to both the larger community and to God.

> Through work that is true to who we are, we share in the work of creation and enter into a continuous process of giving and taking, teaching and learning....Good work releases the divine element in us by which we rediscover the source of our creativity and connection to all living things. (p. 96)

As Soelle suggests, the individual's co-worker relationship with God is a powerful source of creativity and connection. Luther, Soelle, other theologians, and the witness of countless Christians contend that when the individual works as God's co-creator, personal energy revitalizes, obstacles minimize, creativity flows, and a sense of freedom and wholeness predominates, allowing the individual to experience self-transcendence in union with God's purpose. Scripturally, the author of Matthew places this description of human powerfulness in the context of faith, "Nothing will be impossible for you" (Mt 17:20). In vocational terms, this experience might be described as the magnification of gifts.

Returning to Lewis, it is evident that he always had a gift for writing, yet his greatest works were those infused with his Christian identity. Using our two previous examples of Romero and Clare, a similar pattern emerges: call, transformation, and a magnification of gifts beyond what anyone might have predicted. A quiet conservative academic, Romero died a prophet and martyr. Clare, vowed to poverty and obedience, led a cultural revolution for women's spiritual self-determination. By discovering their deepest God-given selves, Romero, Clare, and Lewis unearthed the power of God within themselves to develop personal gifts to the fullest, a magnification that not only enabled them to meet the demands of their specific vocational calls but also to serve the needs of the greater community.

This magnification reveals a final trait of vocational gifts: transparency. When recognized, welcomed, and fully developed, vocational gifts reveal God at work in the world through the efforts of the individual. Having already named gifts as the hands in our anatomy of vocation, we can now add a theological understanding.

The gifts of the individual are, in reality, the hands of God operating in the world. With this insight, it also becomes clear that all gifts, all vocations, have equal value, despite human estimations and qualifications. Lewis himself echoed the words of St. Paul on this topic when he delivered his sermon, "Learning in War-time," in 1939. "The work of a Beethoven and the work of a charwoman become spiritual on precisely the same condition, that of being offered to God, of being done humbly 'as to the Lord.'" He went on to clarify that this fact does not mean that one can ignore the natural gifts and inclinations with which he or she is endowed, but that he or she must, instead, honor the raw material of his or her life.

A mole must dig...and a cock must crow. We are members of one body, but differentiated members, each with his own vocation....In the same confidence that by so doing we are either advancing to the vision of God ourselves or indirectly helping others to do so. (*The Weight of Glory*, p. 56)

Soelle puts it more succinctly, "Through good work we are revealed, in our creative empowerment, as the children of God." In this way, the transparency of vocational gifts teaches us two great truths about authentic Christian identity: God works through our work, and in so doing, brings us closer in union with God.

CHAPTER 6

Community

The final component of our anatomy of vocation is community. Like the skin that both covers and contains the body, community is the skin that defines the shape of vocation and holds the other parts together in a coherent whole while the individual is involved in vocational development. As we have seen in previous chapters, the community is always present in the other parts of vocation's body, interacting with the individual in diverse and important ways. In the case of call, it is often the community itself, whether consciously or unconsciously, that carries or issues the vocational call. Through personal transformation and gifts, the individual is empowered to serve the community in the way that call demands.

Yet this relationship between the individual and the community is not one-sided; it does not require the individual to always be on the giving end. Like human skin that breathes and exchanges nutrients for the good of the body, the vocational skin of community serves the individual too, offering the benefits of others' discernment, wisdom, and direction. Though it can be a source of conflict (a crucial role of the community), community can also provide support and comfort, healing and self-transcendence.

Ultimately, community is both the source and goal of Christian vocation, defining both "who" and "whose" we are.

A Case Study of Community

Dorothy Day was born in Brooklyn, New York, on November 8, 1899. As a young child, she knew the tenement flats and poverty of Chicago's south side and the middle-class suburban comfort of the city's North Side. Depending on her father's journalist employment (or lack thereof), the family moved accordingly. After spending two years on scholarship at the University of Illinois-Urbana, Day dropped out of school in 1916 and moved to New York City where she found a job as a reporter for *The Call*, the city's only Socialist daily. Already socially conscious, Day's work at the paper reinforced her radical political and social leanings, bringing her into contact with labor organizers, revolutionaries, demonstrators, and blue collar workers.

In 1917, she was arrested in Washington, DC, along with a group of other women for protesting the exclusion of women from the electorate. Imprisoned for their actions, the women were mistreated and abused. After staging a hunger strike in the prison, the suffragettes were released by a presidential order, and Day resumed her journalistic efforts, working for *The Masses*, another radical newspaper. A year later, she abandoned writing to train as a nurse in Brooklyn, feeling that journalism was an inadequate response to a world embroiled in war. With the conclusion of the war shortly thereafter, however, she returned to reporting, working in Chicago, New Orleans, and New York, always convinced that the social order was unjust and searching for the ways and means to effect change.

Back in New York in 1924, Day bought a beach cottage on Staten Island and began a four-year common-law marriage with Forster Batterham. Though intellectually and politically suited to each other, Day differed with Batterham on the subject of religion. He was an atheist, while she had come to a deep belief in God. Raised in the Episcopal Church, Day had been increasingly attracted to the Roman Catholic faith as a young radical in New York. When she gave birth in 1927, she had the child baptized in the Catholic Church. Batterham left. By the end of the year, Day too joined the Catholic Church, embracing the gospel as the social directive that would inform her lifework and her very identity.

Five years later, she opened her apartment door to meet Peter Maurin, a former Christian Brother from France who had a radical social vision and had been sent to her by a mutual acquaintance. Together they founded *The Catholic Worker*, the penny-a-copy newspaper that preached the basic gospel values of Catholic social teaching as the means to transform an unjust society. Within six months, the paper produced in Day's kitchen had grown from 2,500 to 100,000 monthly copies. As the voice of Christian social dissent, it challenged urbanization and industrialism and urged its readers to act for change.

Though often unpopular (and even rejected) by the local church and political authorities for her convictions, Day practiced what she preached, offering refuge and assistance to the poor who turned up on her doorstep and unconditional love to her coworkers. Together, Day and Maurin initiated a renewal of the ancient Christian practice of hospitality, founding Catholic Worker houses across the United States to shelter the homeless. Characterized by her critics as unrealistic and anti-establishment, Day's vocation was at one time described as "to comfort the afflicted increasingly and to afflict the comfortable unceasingly" (*Mirrors of God*, p. 4).

In the days prior to World War II, Day became an outspoken advocate for pacifism. She saw the evil of the Nazi rise in Germany, yet supported only the works of mercy, not war. In the 1950s, she was repeatedly jailed for her pacifist stance and other protests against the prevailing social order, believing that the nonviolent way of life was at the heart of the gospel. On her seventy-fifth birthday, she was honored as the individual who best exemplified "the aspiration and action of the American Catholic community during the past forty years" by the Jesuit magazine *America*.

Educated and trained as a journalist, Day's career included stints as a reporter, nursing student, scriptwriter, editor, and activist. After examining the impulses behind her professional endeavors, however, it becomes clear that the welfare of the community—indeed of all persons—was her vocation. While the role of community may not be so apparent or dramatic in our own round of daily tasks, we can still uncover its abiding influence for us personally by taking Day's experience as our model.

The Responsibility of Call

The responsibility of call is a perfect example of the two-way permeability of the vocational skin of community. As we described in Chapter Two, every Christian vocational call is God's invitation to the individual for the purpose of the community. The intention of vocation is for others. Looking at Day's example, we can easily trace her responses to that call, from the early encounters and conversations with other Catholics that she recorded in her autobiography, *The Long Loneliness*, to the evidence of her later testimonies as an opponent of nuclear weaponry.

Throughout her life, Dorothy Day served others. At the same time, the community exercised its responsibility to her by helping to convey that call through the voices and challenges of both articulate, faith-filled Christians and the daily circumstances of the poor and homeless with whom she interacted professionally and personally. Day's relationship with Maurin fueled the activism that defined her greatest contributions to social justice and reform. Yet without the discerning heart of the priest who sent Maurin to meet Day, that relationship may never have happened.

The communal responsibility to assist in discernment of individual vocation is not only a critical component of the theological anatomy of vocation, but seems to be in contemporary times a forgotten one, with the exception of church communities that encourage their members to consider ministry as a calling. Even in those communities, that type of vocational guidance is limited to church ministry roles, ignoring all other types of vocational choices that benefit the human community.

Theologians from all ages—Paul and Luther, Calvin and Soelle, to name only a few—have taken great pains in their instructions to the faithful to regard whatever they do as works of holiness that build up the community when done in the name of God. Yet in a culture that stresses independence and self-fulfillment, many communities have not only abdicated their role in assisting individual discernment, but seem to feel that the role itself is obsolete. As Day's case illustrates, the community's involvement (conscious or not) in helping to call the individual to a specific purpose is central to Christian vocation.

The theological relationship that exists between the individual and the community is characterized by mutuality. Together, the individual and community participate in God's creative work. Recalling that Christian identity is more a question of whose we are than who we are, it becomes even more evident that both the individual and the community bear responsibility to each other for vocational discernment.

Theologian Frederick Buechner takes a different perspective on vocational call, saying it arises in the place where "our deep gladness and the world's deep hunger meet" (*Callings*, p. 13). For Day, the world's deep hunger was a matter of social justice. With the inspiration and direction of Maurin (perhaps chief among the influences in the course of her life), Day found her deep gladness in her radical Christian faith. The resulting combination of that hunger and gladness dictated her lifelong dedication to social reform. Such dedication not only informed and shaped her life but through her agitation and actions, altered the consciousness of both the Catholic Church in America and the nation itself.

The Dynamic of Sacrifice

Like any commitment, vocational dedication requires sacrifice. In his autobiography, Trappist monk Thomas Merton boldly stated this dynamic. "If his vocation is to be really fruitful it must cost him something, and must be a real sacrifice" (*The Seven Storey Mountain*, p. 292). In Day's case, the sacrifices were plentiful and painful, running the gamut from the compromise of everyday convenience (her kitchen table was the editorial desk of *The Catholic Worker*), to the forfeit of an intimate relationship (her loss of Batterham), to personal deprivation and physical abuse (her multiple imprisonments). By choosing to act for her vision of the good of the community, instead of pursuing a path focused on personal needs and wants, Day accepted the suffering that inevitably comes when the individual subjects the personal to the communal. In Christian terms, she chose the way of the cross, suffering for others.

Like the surrender that leads to vocational transformation, however, the sacrifice that is required by the community in every vocation is also a dynamic of empowerment. By giving herself to the will of God, Day allowed God to work powerfully in the world through her. In echoes of St. Clare's experience, Day too found liberation and joy in the midst of her sacrifices as the plans she and Maurin made came to fruition in the Catholic Worker movement. Clinging to her dedication to the gospel, Day championed the Catholic Worker vision of social justice even when she encountered the displeasure of the established Church early in her career. As critic Colman McCarthy remarked in the New Republic, Day had "the wild extreme notion that Christianity is a workable system, the bizarre idea that religion has more to do with what you work at than what you believe" (*Mirrors of God*, p. 4).

Believing that the welfare of her neighbors was her Christian call and duty, Day devoted herself to working for change, despite the personal sacrifices it demanded. Forsaking financial security and a conventional home life in order to accomplish the tasks she saw for herself, Day drove herself physically and mentally to witness to her faith. Perhaps Soelle's words about work can help explain Day's tireless efforts, "Those who come to understand the goal of work as fulfilling the needs of their neighbors tend to experience a transformation in their entire approach to work" (*To Work and To Love*, p. 106). In Day's case, that transformation clearly contributed to her accomplishments for the sake of others, but at the same time demanded personal sacrifice.

Labor may be given, only to be lost as unappreciated, abused by others, or deliberately misinterpreted. It is a great temptation for the individual to abandon vocation. As humans, we seem to naturally crave recognition and desire others to see the meaning we find in our own work. When that doesn't happen, we may begin to falter, often questioning ourselves and the genuineness of the call to which we are responding. Frequently, those who do God's work in controversial or unconventional ways, as Day did, must labor without full support of the community and with only prayer and vision as a resource. This conflict between the individual and the community, one's willingness to be misused and to be a "lost love," this sacrifice of self and work, Martin Luther explained, is the pattern of Christian love. For Day, it was the pattern of her life's work and service.

For Christians, sacrifice and service are bound together in every vocation, theologically as well as practically. No one is a Christian alone, and that truth reveals the reality that every Christian is related to others, woven together in communities of responsibility and love that range from families and friends to all Christians who have gone before. In classic Christian tradition, Day referred to all those she cared for as her brothers and sisters in Christ. Indeed, the fundamental relationship in Christian life is not "me and Jesus" but "we and Jesus." This concept is grounded in the New Testaments' *koinonia*, the Greek word for community. This concept is perhaps as revolutionary now as it was in the first century. It requires practitioners to defy basic human instincts of self-interest and move beyond even self-transcendence to a contemplation and action focused on others. It requires the dying to self proclaimed by Jesus Christ in word and on the cross of Calvary.

Yet it is precisely here, in self-dying and in community building, that there is assurance that every person has a vocation. In community, every person has a purpose. As part of community, the individual listens for call and discernment, not just from within but from without as well, allowing the community to voice God's word. In Luther's terms, it is whatever the hand finds to do, recognizing that the circumstances—even those of conflict—are also the work of God, crafted amidst community and designed as divine opportunity to participate in God's ongoing creative work.

Wholeness in Community

Sacrifice, while essential to the fullness of vocational development, is not the last word in the relationship between the individual and the community. As the cross of Jesus demonstrates, resurrection is the last word. Before her death, Dorothy Day was recognized for her extraordinary achievements on behalf of both the poor and the gospel itself, winning public accolades and even international support. Loved deeply by the many people whose lives she affected, Day's work continues to thrive in Catholic Worker houses, soup kitchens, and public assistance programs all around the United States.

Though often criticized about the coherence of her "wild extreme notion," Day herself knew the new life it could offer to a suffering society and brought that awareness back to the attention of her coworkers through the pages of The Catholic Worker. On a personal level, her vocation renewed her own life, giving her the direction and arena she needed in which to develop her vocational gifts and fulfill her God-given call. By combining her actions with her deepest beliefs, she achieved a powerful integration of life and spirit that yielded a wholeness for herself and the wider community.

Thomas Merton named this paradox of contemplation and action as the "hidden wholeness" that lies just beneath the surface of our lives (*The Active Life*, p. 29). As the experiences of Day, Lewis, Clare, and Romero suggest, individuals who seek and develop Christian vocations may, in actuality, be accessing their wholeness. From this perspective we might infer that vocation, then, is not only God's intention for us to serve others but also God's intention for us to achieve wholeness. It is a wholeness integral to our spiritual and temporal selves, a wholeness that heals the woundedness of our sacrifices, a wholeness that unites us to others and to God. In the process of realizing our own particular vocation—grounded, defined, and enabled by community—we truly become ourselves and God's.

CHAPTER 7

Passion

As we have seen, call, transformation, gifts, and community are the distinct, yet interrelated, components that form the body of Christian vocation. Each element makes an essential and unique contribution to the whole. At the same time, each supports every other element with the conditions or resources vital to its functioning. In the case of vocation, the whole is truly greater than the sum of its parts. For when vocation is realized and lived, the cumulative effect of call, transformation, gifts, and community allows Christians not only to realize God's particular purpose but to actually share in the life of God.

Yet our theological model of the body of vocation is still inadequate. Just as a physical body requires blood to bring it to life, so too does the body of Christian vocation require an animating principle to bring it to life in every person's experience. Fortunately, we already have encountered this principle, this lifeblood, in each of our case studies, as well as in the experience of Jesus himself. The blood of the body of vocation is passion.

The Animating Principle

Just as the authentic meaning of vocation has been buried beneath layers of interpretation, the original meaning of passion has been obscured frequently, if not ignored altogether, by popular usage. Most typically referenced in a context of sexuality, love, emotions, or even obsession, the word "passion" comes from the Latin *passio,* or suffering, a meaning that is integral to the role of passion in vocation. According to *Webster's New Collegiate Dictionary,* passion can either be "the state or capacity of being acted on by external agents or forces" or an intense emotion (as distinguished from reason) that compels action. Understood in this way, passion combines receiving and giving, passive and active, weakness and strength. Our exposition of passion here will find these meanings evident in the arena of vocation, leading to deeper appreciation and recognition of this vocational life-blood as well as to the beginnings of a theology of passion.

Passion and Call

In our case studies of Romero, Clare, Lewis, and Day, passion is clearly present in each person's vocational experience. Romero was reluctant to take a public stand against the injustices inflicted on the poor. Despite firsthand witness of oppression, Romero opted to avoid conflict with religious superiors who sanctioned the status quo. Heeding their expectations and directives, he blocked any response he might have made that would be contrary to their wishes.

Bound by his oath of obedience, Romero was subservient to his superiors until the death of his friend galvanized him into action. Grieving and shaken to his core, Romero suddenly found himself in a new place, spiritually and emotionally, which allowed him to open the gates of his love for the people he shepherded. In that experience, he shed the personal safety and security of his previous conformity for a call to prophet and martyr. In casting aside his instincts for political, ecclesial, and even physical survival, he accessed the deepest power of his vocational call and found a passion that obliterated personal boundaries and expectations—transforming him and his ministry.

Romero's biographers and friends repeatedly remarked on the depth of his passion for his flock, citing his compassion as a primary force in his ministry.

> Moved by compassion, he began to feel the fire of righteous anger in his soul…he was "pulled" forward into a holiness which he had not anticipated but which he discovered in the people's call and the demands of history. (*Oscar Romero*, p. 12)

The use of terms of movement—"moved" and "pulled"—in describing Romero's experience of his vocational call is not only insightful and revelatory but confirms our earlier observations on the nature of vocational passion. For Romero, passion was indeed a force that compelled action, a force that moved him. As his story testifies, the passion that simultaneously liberated and engulfed him was irresistible. Freed, yet overwhelmed by this passion, Romero discovered in it God's particular call to him, investing that call with an authority that only increased its power in his life.

At the same time, the perception that Romero was pulled reveals an opposing, difficult truth about passion. It demands a certain vulnerability on the part of the individual, requiring one to submit to the agency of others. In terms of vocation, that particular agent is God. Yet it is also evident that God does not always announce himself as the originating agency, leaving it up to the individual to make the choice to risk vulnerability or strengthen defenses. Romero, moved and pulled by his passion, saw and accepted this demand of vulnerability as the cost of his ministry.

> Anyone committed to the poor must suffer the same fate as the poor. And in El Salvador we know the fate of the poor: to be taken away, to be tortured, to be jailed, to be found dead. (*The Violence of Love*, p. 192)

For Romero, passion encompassed suffering, power, and weakness as he responded to his vocational call.

Passion and Transformation

In the course of her life, and particularly in the experience of her vocational transformation, Clare of Assisi, too, was intimately acquainted with the effect of passion. Known by her friends and associates as a woman who was deeply, intensely in love with God, Clare gave herself over to that passion, letting it lead her wherever it might.

From the moment of her clandestine departure from her family home, to her tumultuous confrontation with her father as he attempted to retrieve her, Clare clung to her passion, successfully resisting the claims anyone or anything else might have had upon her. Seen in this light, Clare's passion was unmistakably destructive, tearing down the societal, familial, and religious barriers that had restrained it from its fullest expression. At the same time, this deconstruction effected by passion was also creative as it laid open Clare's life to new possibilities and an as-yet-unimagined future. Set loose from what had been, she was free to see and create what might be.

For the historical person of Clare, however, this destructive/creative duality of passion was not initially a source of confidence and reassurance in the concrete circumstances of her daily existence. On the contrary, neither Clare nor Francis quite knew what to do with her evolving vocational transformation. After a brief stay in the Benedictine convent in which Francis placed her, Clare found herself (and her passion) still unsatisfied. Again rejecting the form that bound her, Clare, driven by her passion, sought a new shape for her vowed life, and spent the rest of her life securing it in the foundation of her own order.

Like Romero, Clare was pulled and moved by passion beyond the safe confines of accepted and expected behaviors and attitudes to explore new personal territory. Those who knew Clare saw a transformation fueled by passion. In Haughton's terms, Clare and Romero experienced the passionate breakthrough—violent, life-changing—that brought them the possibility of a personal whole-ness they had not previously known, a wholeness to which God called them through their vocations.

Passion and Gifts

The relationship between passion and wholeness is especially evident in the purpose of vocational gifts. Our study of C.S. Lewis often returned to the concept of passion—passion as embodied by personal interests, passion as significant to vocational direction and discernment, passion as a source of meaning and path to personal wholeness. That these aspects of passion were present in his vocational gifts was not coincidental. Understood as gifts from God, we also understand these gifts to have God-given purpose. Yet, as we have seen, many gifts do not achieve their fullest expression until later in a person's development, leaving those same gifts languishing in varying stages of visibility (or invisibility). It is the work of passion to bring those gifts to the awareness of the individual and invest them with both an attractiveness and authority that demands recognition and response.

In Lewis' case, attraction seemed to happen early and naturally before any barriers could erect themselves to interfere with his gift development. It might even be suggested that the death of his mother while he was still a child disposed him to seek solace in his imaginative play to a greater degree than if his mother had been present. Encouraged by his brother, his teachers, and later his friends, to nurture his literary gifts, Lewis thrived artistically and creatively, welcoming the new directions to which he was called, be they commitments to correspondence, public address, or personal mentoring. In this way, passion led Lewis to a wholeness through his gifts and their development.

It is intriguing (and significant) to note that the passion that animated Lewis' work and drew him to wholeness, the passion to which he gave voice, literally and literarily, ultimately voiced God. In his fiction, Lewis wrote about Christian faith. In his sermons, he preached about human nature and God. In his friendships, he was guided by Christian sensibilities. Passion acts to achieve a divine purpose, to reveal God through the individual's gifts.

Passion and Community

Day's passions also brought her Christian vocation to life and in turn, voiced God. As she reported in her autobiography, she was always deeply affected by the people around her. When her father lost his job during her childhood and the family was forced to move into an impoverished part of the city, she identified with her neighbors—an identification that grew into a lifelong solidarity with the poor. As a young radical, she sought affirmation and companionship among others who advocated social change, all the while feeling unsettled and alone in the world.

Upon her conversion to Catholicism, Day irrevocably bound herself to the Christian community and by so doing, found a new foundation for her passion for social justice—the gospel. Powered by this passion, she dedicated herself to changing the lot of the poor through her community activism and gospel witness, often enduring the hardships and suffering that mark the deepest passion. Yet in the course of her career, she also rattled the conscience and consciousness of the greater human community by challenging others to heed Jesus' commands to do the work of God in bringing about God's reign on earth.

One of the best lessons we can learn from Day is that personal passion is a formidable force in an individual's life and is likewise an impressive—even irresistible—agent in the life of the wider community. Historically and concretely, God works through individuals to affect communities.

Using human hands, bodies, language, and emotions, God's work begins in one person and, through passion, commands the involvement of others, until the ripple effect of that passion spreads throughout the whole community. As our studies of Day, Romero, Clare, and Lewis have demonstrated, passion is the blood that pumps life into the body of vocation, enabling it to be the effective instrument of God. If we acknowledge that vocations are God's purpose for our lives, the passion of vocation is more than an animating principle. It is, in truth, God's own voice in intimate communication with the individual.

The Passion of Our Lord

Just as we used the experience of Jesus to validate our theological anatomy of vocation, we can turn to the scriptural record to verify our conclusions about vocational passion. Unlike the artistic representations of a serene Jesus that many Christians remember from their childhood, the Jesus portrayed in the New Testament is a passionate man. Again and again, he is characterized by the gospel authors as a man who feels deeply and gives voice to strong emotion. His reactions run from anger to tenderness, from grief to wrenching agony. He speaks sharply in frustration when his disciples fail to drive a demon out, lamenting "You faithless generation, how much longer must I be among you? How much longer must I put up with you?" (Mk 9:19). He curses a fig tree for its lack of fruit and curses the Pharisees for their hypocrisy and wreaks havoc among the sellers in the Temple.

Speaking and teaching with authority and power, Jesus heals the multitudes and condemns the unrepentant. Driven by his mission, he risks the opposition of powerful enemies, courts the censorship of his own religious community, and invites arrest and ultimately death. Yet he is not unaware of his increasing vulnerability as he moves toward Jerusalem. Several times he warns his disciples of the terrible climax awaiting him, yet he accepts the cost of his work. His "breakthrough," to use Haughton's language, beckons him forward. Fueled by his passion—a passion revealed even in his youth as he remained in Jerusalem with the teachers in the temple—Jesus does the work he finds at hand, among his neighbors, his enemies, strangers, or acquaintances. Filled with the Spirit, he does the work of his Father, laboring to make a new creation for all people.

Some scholars, like William R. Herzog, II, make a strong case for naming the work of the historical Jesus as prophet of the justice of the reign of God—a justice sought through the liberation of the oppressed from imposed structures and systems that separated humans from God (*Jesus, Justice, and the Reign of God*, p. 47). Other scholars debate the mission of Jesus as a ministry of healing, teaching, or revolution. Despite their differing perspectives, however, scholars admit that every study of the Jesus found in the New Testament is colored by the author's personal christology, or as Herzog puts it, "it is impossible to study the historical Jesus without doing theology" (p. xii). Be that as it may, the inescapable fact is that every gospel records the culminating expression of Jesus' vocation, as the passion of our Lord.

The use of the word "passion" is by no means arbitrary or insignificant. Using the original Latin for "suffering," the passion explicitly details the physical and spiritual suffering of Jesus. As the climax of his earthly work, the passion is also an apt summation, for Jesus had passion for God and passion for God's people. Fittingly, the act of his life that achieved his purpose was passion incarnate. In his agony and death, all the characteristics of passion converged: surrender, vulnerability, suffering, power, self-transcendence, and transformation.

The result of his Passion was, indeed, a new creation—eternal life for all those who believe in his resurrection. Especially pertinent to our vocational theology, however, is the observation that in his passion/Passion, Jesus not only heard God's voice and realized

God's purpose for his life but fully incarnated God as proclaimed by the guards in Matthew 27:54, "Truly this man was God's Son!"

Keeping that in mind, the question we need to now address is do we, as Christians, likewise "incarnate" God when we embrace our vocational passion?

A Theology of Vocation

In order to answer this question, a review of what we have already said might prove helpful.

Historically and experientially, we have found that Christian vocation is both a theological concept and a lived reality, grounded in the example of Jesus. Initiated by God, vocation is the specific call to the individual to fulfill a purpose to benefit the community. Shaped by the particular circumstances of one's life, vocation is uniquely tailored to each individual. More than simply a job or career path, vocation takes into account the whole person, integrating spirituality, lived experiences, relationships, the material world, and ongoing self-discovery and growth.

In the course of vocational development, the Christian can expect to experience personal transformation that includes both sacrifice and the fruition of gifts. When fully realized in the life of the individual, vocation is revealed to be self-transcending as the effects of personal vocation reach beyond the individual to act upon the community. In this way, the Christian works cooperatively with the creative will of God to accomplish the good of the community while at the same time being invited to spiritual wholeness.

The purpose-driven body of vocation comes to life through passion. Though it may escape discernment by the individual during youth or even later years, once recognized and accepted, vocational passion demands the adult Christian's attention and response. When passion focuses the call of vocation, it carries with it an undeniable authority in one's life.

In each case study, we have seen the role passion has played in establishing and furthering vocation. Romero's passion for the oppressed poured out in his call as prophet; Clare's passion for God transformed her; Lewis' passion for stories made him an exceptional teacher; Day's passion for her neighbor gave new meaning to community. Upon closer examination and reflection, we can also see that the passion in each individual's life not only informed, transformed, and endowed their particular vocations, but over time conformed the people themselves more closely to the example of Jesus in the way they gave of themselves for others. Romero was martyred; Clare devoted herself to the care of her sisters; Lewis was dedicated to spreading the gospel; Day spent her life seeking justice for the poor.

Understood from this perspective, every passion that contributes to Christian vocation ultimately carries the potential for the individual to embody Christ. If we believe Jesus' own words, "whoever welcomes me welcomes not me but the one who sent me" (Mk 9:37), we find both the answer to our question and the affirmation of vocation. We do, indeed, incarnate God when we embrace our vocational passion.

Yet a caveat must be appended to this answer. As Christians, we believe we are in need of the redemption Jesus Christ alone accomplished for us. Consequently, even our most earnest attempts to do God's will or realize our vocation will fall short of perfection. We might best comprehend vocational development as a duality that holds together in a reciprocal tension the fullness of God and the incompleteness of the individual, a duality that reflects the eschatological dichotomy of the reign of God being simultaneously now and not-yet.

In simpler terms, Martin Luther explained this vocational tension as "we go now this way and now that," demonstrating the natural human weaknesses that leave gaps—albeit unintentional and unavoidable—between purpose and practice. In Luther's theology, however, it is in these gaps that we find God working on the individual, making vocation not only the way we embody God but the way in which God works on or sanctifies the individual ("Luther on Vocation," p. 5). Recalling that passion is the animating principle of vocation, we might even speculate that one's vocational passions are actually God's own urgings to bring the Christian into the divine embrace.

Seen in this light, Christian vocation is the expression of the mutual passion of and between the individual and God. As Christ modeled for us (and our case studies affirmed), this passionate embrace identified as vocation is life-changing and ultimately world-changing, whether on the small scale of our immediate relationships and environment or on the larger scale of community, nation, or world. No matter the stage or setting, Christian vocation reveals God at work in and through the individual, affirming both who and whose we are.

CHAPTER 8

While describing the anatomy of vocation has been primarily a theological task, we would be greatly mistaken if we failed to examine the spiritual implications of this theology in the contemporary experience of Christians. After all, vocation is, as we repeatedly have found, more than simply grounded in the details of daily life. It is the dynamic interaction of all the elements of each person's experience responding to God's call to purpose on behalf of others.

Characterized this way, vocation is about tangible matters and practical consideration. It is about the way we live and why we live that way. Rich or poor, clerk or CEO, homemaker or businessperson, theologian or laborer, employed or not, all Christians are called to vocation right where they live. In this final chapter, our goal is to access academic elements of our theology of vocation and translate them into practical applications from which every Christian can benefit.

Christian Vocation

Christian vocation is God's call to the individual to the service of others. As a theological concept, it focuses on the revelation of God at work in and through the individual to move forward the great and ongoing enterprise of creation. On a personal level, vocation is about the individual's role in that creative process. Contrary to popular belief, vocation is not about the standards or expectations of secular society or about self-development or personal achievement. Instead, Christian vocation is counter-cultural, offering an alternate set of values to those championed by the predominant culture. Rather than self-interest, the interest of others sets the vocational agenda. In this way, Christians follow in the footsteps of Jesus to accomplish God's purpose on earth.

Three conclusions flow directly from this brief summation of Christian vocation:

1. God gives each person a vocation;

2. the purpose of Christian vocation is to serve others; and

3. vocation gives meaning to life.

God gives each person a vocation. Called by name, every Christian has a personal relationship with God. With relationship comes responsibility. Though the description of our particular responsibility or purpose may not be spelled out for us on a well-lit marquee, that does not excuse us from finding and fulfilling our vocation.

The purpose of Christian vocation is to serve others. Christians know God through the witness of others, beginning with Jesus and continuing through the ages to the present day. "Love your neighbor" is second only to the command to love God. When we search for ways to love our neighbor, we inevitably arrive at ways to serve others.

Vocation gives meaning to life. Participating with God in the ongoing work of creation is both the obligation and privilege of the Christian. Every individual has a unique role to play in this cooperative act. Those who co-create with God change the world. Those who refuse, impoverish both themselves and others.

The Body of Vocation

Call is the head and heart of vocation. Grounded in the circumstances, relationships, and experiences of one's life, God's call can vary from the whisper of a passing thought to the thunder of a life-changing moment. For most, hearing a particular call requires readiness, openness, and patience. For some people, it entails conflict and painful self-examination. Vocational call is characterized by authority, insistence, and passion, and over time becomes irresistible for the Christian. Vocational calls may come at any time in all shapes, sizes, and volumes, but they are shaped out of our own life experiences.

Transformation is the body that moves vocation forward. Once the individual has responded to call, the Christian experiences a personal change. Like call, transformation actually may manifest itself slowly over time (much like flowing water reshaping a rock), or it may happen dramatically and very visibly. The timing of transformation is the God-given opportunity for personal breakthrough to new abilities and consciousness.

Regardless of the pace, transformation alters the individual's perspective and enlarges personal horizons and often includes periods of struggle or surrender as the individual overcomes barriers to continuing growth. However, the emotional, physical, and spiritual energy expended in this endeavor is not lost. It results in freedom and empowerment for the individual to fulfill the demands of one's particular vocation. When we are challenged by life's circumstances, God is already at work on and with us to effect transformation.

Gifts are the hands of vocation. They are the means we have (and that God uses) to achieve purpose. Called personally by God, every Christian has particular skills, abilities, aptitudes, and attitudes that God intends for the service of others. Some gifts are easily recognized and received; others may require nurturing. The identification of gifts can come in many ways: individual reflection and prayer, communal assistance and observation, mentoring and spiritual direction. In some people's experience, naming and accepting personal gifts offers concrete vocational direction and reveals call itself. The dynamic effect that the different parts of the body of vocation can exert upon each other demonstrates the interrelationship that exists among those parts. For the Christian, gifts become fully developed, operative, and meaningful in the context of realized vocation. By learning to know, respect, and develop our unique gifts, we can cooperate with God in our vocational purpose.

Community Gives Definition

Community is the skin of vocation, holding together parts of the body as it gives definition to every particular vocational purpose. As support for the individual, community plays an active role in vocational development, issuing call, precipitating personal transformation, and discerning gifts. At times, the community challenges the individual Christian through conflict to grow and transcend personal limitations. In the act of sacrifice, the Christian models the example of Jesus who gave up self-interest for the good of the community. Such sacrifice is the defining characteristic of Christian vocation, and through self-transcendence, sacrifice paradoxically allows the individual to attain a personal wholeness that integrates both the spiritual and temporal aspects of human nature. Sacrifice is the hallmark of our Christian vocation.

Passion is the animating principle of vocation, the life-blood that makes vocation a real-world experience for the Christian. Flowing in and through the body of vocation we can find passion in every part—call, transformation, gifts, and community. In vocational passions, we discover irresistible attractions that subtly shape or forcefully form our responses to God's call.

In transformation, passion is the energy that fuels both surrender and breakthrough to liberation and empowerment. Quite often, passion comes to the Christian in the gifts God grants, and in the exercise of these gifts, the individual serves the community via a particular vocational purpose. At the same time, through that purpose, the Christian contributes to creation as co-worker with God. In this way, God leads the Christian through passion to vocational fulfillment, personal wholeness, and ultimately, the Divine embrace. Passion is the way God reveals, develops, and fulfills vocational purpose in each Christian. Through passion we are joined to God.

Vocation, then, is the path every Christian can follow to God. Perfectly modeled by Jesus, vocation is the work we do to move God's creative enterprise forward by giving ourselves for others. Regardless of the name of the task—day-care provider, doctor, data-entry operator, minister, or farmer—it is our contribution to God's great work. Knowing this, our theology of vocation also requires us to honor others and the work they do, for both the contributions they make to our own vocations and for their unique purposes as well. As Paul taught, we are all one body, affecting each other in all we do.

Perhaps an appreciation for the people, places, and circumstances of our lives is fundamental to developing even a rudimentary vocational awareness. The best vocational advice comes from Paul's words to the Thessalonians, "Rejoice always, pray without ceasing, give thanks in all circumstances; for this is the will of God in Christ Jesus for you" (1 Thess 5:16–18). Almost two thousand years later, these words are still sound advice for every Christian, especially when we recognize that the people, the places, and the circumstances of our lives yield to us our purpose, our passion, and our vocation. Through them, we grow in the likeness of Jesus and are drawn closer to God.

Bibliography

Armstrong, Regis, ed. *Clare of Assisi: Early Documents*. Mahwah, NJ: Paulist Press, 1988.

Armstrong, Regis and Ignatius Brady. *Francis and Clare: The Complete Works*. Mahwah, NJ: Paulist Press, 1982.

Bainton, Roland. *The Reformation of the Sixteenth Century*. Boston: Beacon Press, 1985.

Bates, Charles. *Pigs Eat Wolves*. St Paul, MN: Yes International Publishers, 1991.

Calhoun, Robert Lowry. *God and the Common Life*. New York: Charles Scribner's Sons, 1935.

Daniel-Rops, Henri. *The Call of St. Clare*. New York: Hawthorn Books, Inc., 1963.

Day, Dorothy. *The Long Loneliness*. New York: Curtis Books, 1952.

Dennis, Marie, Renny Golden, and Scott Wright. *Oscar Romero: Reflections on His Life and Writings*. Maryknoll: Orbis Books, 2000.

DeRobeck, Nesta. *Clare of Assisi*. Milwaukee: Bruce Publishing Co., 1951.

Fowler, James W. *Stages of Faith*. New York: HarperCollins, 1981.

Gardner, Howard. *Leading Minds.* New York: Basic Books, 1995.

Goetz, Joseph W. *Mirrors of God.* Cincinnati: St. Anthony Messenger Press, 1984.

Haughton, Rosemary. *The Passionate God.* New York: Paulist Press, 1981.

Herzog, William R., III. *Jesus, Justice, and the Reign of God.* Louisville: Westminster John Knox Press, 2000.

Hodgson, Irene, trans. *Archbishop Oscar Romero: A Shepherd's Diary.* Cincinnati: St. Anthony Messenger Press, 1993.

Hollenbach, David, SJ. *Nuclear Ethics: A Christian Moral Argument.* New York: Paulist Press, 1983.

Johnston, William. *The Mirror Mind.* San Francisco: Harper & Row, 1981.

Kolden, Marc. "Luther on Vocation." *Word & World,* Vol. III, No. 4, Luther Seminary, 1983.

Levoy, Gregg. *Callings: Finding and Following an Authentic Life.* New York: Three Rivers Press, 1997.

Lewis, C.S. *The Weight of Glory.* New York: HarperCollins, 2001.

—. *Surprised by Joy.* New York: Harcourt, Brace & World, 1955.

Meeks, Wayne A. *The Origins of Christian Morality.* New Haven: Yale University, 1993.

Meisel, Anthony and M.L. del Mastro, trans. *The Rule of St. Benedict.* New York: Doubleday, 1975.

Merton, Thomas. *The Seven Storey Mountain: A Autobiography of Faith.* San Diego: Harcourt Brace Jovanovich, Inc., 1948.

Palmer, Parker. *The Active Life: A Spirituality of Work, Creativity, and Caring.* San Francisco: Harper & Row, 1990.

—. *Let Your Life Speak.* San Francisco: Jossey-Bass, 2000.

Peterson, Ingrid. *Clare of Assisi: A Biographical Study.* Quincy, IL:

Franciscan Press, 1993.

Powell, Mark Allan. *Jesus as a Figure in History*. Louisville: Westminster John Knox Press, 1998.

Romero, Oscar. *The Violence of Love*. Farmington, PA: The Plough Publishing House, 1998.

Sellner, Edward C. *Mentoring*. Cambridge, MA: Cowley Publications, 2002.

—. "Work." *New Dictionary of Catholic Spirituality*. Michael Downey, ed. Collegeville, MN: Liturgical Press, 1993.

Senior, Donald, ed. *New American Bible*. Oxford: Oxford University Press, Inc., 1990.

Sobrino, Jon, SJ. *Archbishop Romero: Memories and Reflections*. Maryknoll, NY: Orbis Books, 1990.

Soelle, Dorothee and Shirley Cloyes. *To Work and To Love: A Theology of Creation*. Philadelphia: Fortress Press, 1984.

Spohn, William C. *Go and Do Likewise*. New York: Continuum Publishing, 2000.

Stone, Irving. *Dear Theo: The Autobiography of Vincent van Gogh*. New York: Penguin Books, 1995.

Whyte, David. *Crossing the Unknown Sea: Work as a Pilgrimage of Identity*. New York: Riverhead Books, 2001.

Wingren, Gustaf. *Luther on Vocation*. Philadelphia: Muhlenberg Press, 1957.